OPPOSING VIEWPOINTS® SERIES

Global Sustainability

Other Books of Related Interest:

Opposing Viewpoints Series

Endangered Oceans

The Environment

Natural Gas

At Issue Series

Biofuels

Fracking

What Is the Impact of Green Practices?

Wind Farms

Current Controversies Series

Gasoline

Global Warming

Oil Spills

"Congress shall make no law ... abridging the freedom of speech, or of the press."

First Amendment to the US Constitution

The basic foundation of our democracy is the First Amendment guarantee of freedom of expression. The Opposing Viewpoints series is dedicated to the concept of this basic freedom and the idea that it is more important to practice it than to enshrine it.

338.9
G562

OPPOSING
VIEWPOINTS®
SERIES

Global Sustainability

Dedria Bryfonski, Book Editor

GREENHAVEN PRESS
A part of Gale, Cengage Learning

GALE
CENGAGE Learning·

Farmington Hills, Mich • San Francisco • New York • Waterville, Maine
Meriden, Conn • Mason, Ohio • Chicago

GALE
CENGAGE Learning

Judy Galens, *Manager, Frontlist Acquisitions*

© 2016 Greenhaven Press, a part of Gale, Cengage Learning.

Gale and Greenhaven Press are registered trademarks used herein under license.

For more information, contact:
Greenhaven Press
27500 Drake Rd.
Farmington Hills, MI 48331-3535
Or you can visit our Internet site at gale.cengage.com

For product information and technology assistance, contact us at

Gale Customer Support, 1-800-877-4253
For permission to use material from this text or product, submit all requests online at www.cengage.com/permissions

Further permissions questions can be emailed to permissionrequest@cengage.com

Articles in Greenhaven Press anthologies are often edited for length to meet page requirements. In addition, original titles of these works are changed to clearly present the main thesis and to explicitly indicate the author's opinion. Every effort is made to ensure that Greenhaven Press accurately reflects the original intent of the authors. Every effort has been made to trace the owners of copyrighted material.

Cover Image copyright © violetkaipa/Shutterstock.com.

LIBRARY OF CONGRESS CATALOGING-IN-PUBLICATION DATA

Names: Bryfonski, Dedria, editor.
Title: Global sustainability / Dedria Bryfonski, book editor.
Description: Farmington Hills, Mich. : Greenhaven Press, a part of Gale, Cengage Learning, [2016] | Series: Opposing viewpoints | Includes bibliographical references and index.
Identifiers: LCCN 2015029478| ISBN 9780737775204 (hardcover) | ISBN 9780737775211 (pbk.)
Subjects: LCSH: Sustainability. | Genetically modified foods. | Water supply. | Equality. | Economic development.
Classification: LCC HC79.E5 G59147 2016 | DDC 338.9/27--dc23
LC record available at http://lccn.loc.gov/2015029478

Printed in the United States of America
1 2 3 4 5   20 19 18 17 16

Contents

Chapter 3: Does Social Equity Promote Global Sustainability?

Chapter 4: Is Economic Growth Compatible with Sustainability?

Why Consider Opposing Viewpoints?

> "The only way in which a human being can make some approach to knowing the whole of a subject is by hearing what can be said about it by persons of every variety of opinion and studying all modes in which it can be looked at by every character of mind. No wise man ever acquired his wisdom in any mode but this."
>
> John Stuart Mill

In our media-intensive culture it is not difficult to find differing opinions. Thousands of newspapers and magazines and dozens of radio and television talk shows resound with differing points of view. The difficulty lies in deciding which opinion to agree with and which "experts" seem the most credible. The more inundated we become with differing opinions and claims, the more essential it is to hone critical reading and thinking skills to evaluate these ideas. Opposing Viewpoints books address this problem directly by presenting stimulating debates that can be used to enhance and teach these skills. The varied opinions contained in each book examine many different aspects of a single issue. While examining these conveniently edited opposing views, readers can develop critical thinking skills such as the ability to compare and contrast authors' credibility, facts, argumentation styles, use of persuasive techniques, and other stylistic tools. In short, the Opposing Viewpoints Series is an ideal way to attain the higher-level thinking and reading skills so essential in a culture of diverse and contradictory opinions.

In addition to providing a tool for critical thinking, Opposing Viewpoints books challenge readers to question their own strongly held opinions and assumptions. Most people form their opinions on the basis of upbringing, peer pressure, and personal, cultural, or professional bias. By reading carefully balanced opposing views, readers must directly confront new ideas as well as the opinions of those with whom they disagree. This is not to argue simplistically that everyone who reads opposing views will—or should—change his or her opinion. Instead, the series enhances readers' understanding of their own views by encouraging confrontation with opposing ideas. Careful examination of others' views can lead to the readers' understanding of the logical inconsistencies in their own opinions, perspective on why they hold an opinion, and the consideration of the possibility that their opinion requires further evaluation.

Evaluating Other Opinions

To ensure that this type of examination occurs, Opposing Viewpoints books present all types of opinions. Prominent spokespeople on different sides of each issue as well as well-known professionals from many disciplines challenge the reader. An additional goal of the series is to provide a forum for other, less known, or even unpopular viewpoints. The opinion of an ordinary person who has had to make the decision to cut off life support from a terminally ill relative, for example, may be just as valuable and provide just as much insight as a medical ethicist's professional opinion. The editors have two additional purposes in including these less known views. One, the editors encourage readers to respect others' opinions—even when not enhanced by professional credibility. It is only by reading or listening to and objectively evaluating others' ideas that one can determine whether they are worthy of consideration. Two, the inclusion of such viewpoints encourages the important critical thinking skill of objectively evaluating an author's credentials and bias. This evaluation will illuminate an author's reasons for taking a particular stance on an issue and will aid in readers' evaluation of the author's ideas.

It is our hope that these books will give readers a deeper understanding of the issues debated and an appreciation of the complexity of even seemingly simple issues when good and honest people disagree. This awareness is particularly important in a democratic society such as ours in which people enter into public debate to determine the common good. Those with whom one disagrees should not be regarded as enemies but rather as people whose views deserve careful examination and may shed light on one's own.

Thomas Jefferson once said that "difference of opinion leads to inquiry, and inquiry to truth." Jefferson, a broadly educated man, argued that "if a nation expects to be ignorant and free . . . it expects what never was and never will be." As individuals and as a nation, it is imperative that we consider the opinions of others and examine them with skill and discernment. The Opposing Viewpoints series is intended to help readers achieve this goal.

David L. Bender and Bruno Leone,
Founders

Introduction

> "Humanity has the ability to make devel-
> opment sustainable to ensure that it
> meets the needs of the present without
> compromising the ability of future gen-
> erations to meet their own needs."
> —United Nations,
> "Report of the World Commission
> on Environment and Development:
> Our Common Future," 1987

On the New York Public Library's list of the top twenty-
five books that changed history is Rachel Carson's *Silent
Spring.* Published in 1962, *Silent Spring* details how the insecticide DDT (dichlorodiphenyltrichloroethane) accumulates in
the fatty tissues of humans and animals, causing cancer and
genetic damage. The book is generally credited with launching
the environmental movement in the United States.

Throughout the 1960s, the environmental movement
gained strength as concerns grew over pollution, the threat of
nuclear radiation, and the destruction of entire ecosystems
around the globe. Spurred by the Swedish delegation to the
United Nations (UN), the first United Nations Conference on
the Human Environment (UNCHE) was held in Stockholm in
1972. UNCHE was important because it put environmental issues on the international agenda for the first time. In addition
to raising awareness of the environment, the conference resulted in the establishment of the United Nations Environment Programme, an international organization with the aim
of coordinating global efforts to promote sustainability and
protect the environment. The conference produced the Stockholm Declaration, which established principles for such environmental issues as human rights, natural resource manage-

ment, pollution prevention, and the relationship between the environment and development.

Ten years later, it was apparent that little progress had been made in protecting the environment. Concerned about the rapid deterioration, the UN established a World Commission on Environment and Development and appointed as chair Gro Harlem Brundtland, the former prime minister of Norway. It was in the commission's report, published in 1987 as "Our Common Future," also known as the Brundtland Report, that the term "sustainable development" was first defined.

Two years after "Our Common Future" was published, the United Nations was convinced that environmental matters were worsening rather than improving. The UN General Assembly stated it was "deeply concerned by the continuing deterioration of the state of the environment and the serious degradation of the global life-support systems, as well as by trends that, if allowed to continue, could disrupt the global ecological balance, jeopardize the life-sustaining qualities of the earth and lead to an ecological catastrophe." The UN called for a conference on environment and development to be held in Rio de Janeiro, Brazil, in 1992 that would create strategies and measures to halt and reverse the effects of environmental degradation and promote sustainable development in all countries. The largest ever environmental conference, the Earth Summit, was attended by 108 heads of state and representatives from 172 countries. The conference marked the first international effort to establish action plans and strategies around the concept of sustainable development. The message of the summit was that governments need to rethink their current approach to economic development so as to halt the destruction of natural resources and the pollution of the planet. As a result of the Earth Summit, the United Nations set up the UN Commission on Sustainable Development to monitor progress toward the established goals.

The Rio conference, which increased awareness of the need for sustainable development and secured high-level political commitment to environmental protection, was largely considered a success.

With the purpose of discussing the role of the United Nations in the new millennium, the Millennium Summit was held in September 2000 in New York City. Attended by 149 heads of state and high-ranking officials from more than forty other countries, the summit committed nations to a new global partnership to reduce extreme poverty and set out a series of time-bound targets, with a deadline of 2015, which have become known as the Millennium Development Goals (MDGs).

In 2002 the World Summit on Sustainable Development was held in Johannesburg, South Africa, to adopt concrete steps and identify quantifiable targets to better implement the goals of the 1992 Earth Summit. In contrast to the Rio conference, the 2002 summit was marked by controversy and its results are generally regarded to be disappointing. Then US president George W. Bush did not attend the summit, and the United States delegation successfully lobbied to have global warming removed from the agenda.

One of the disappointments of the summit was its failure to adopt a numerical goal for the amount of energy to be obtained by renewable sources. A compromise was reached that endorsed increased reliance on renewables without establishing targets on goals such as boosting renewable and green sources like solar and wind power. Some believed the most positive outcome of the summit was the agreement to halve the number of people lacking clean drinking water and basic sanitation by 2015.

In 2012 the United Nations held another conference in Rio de Janeiro to mark the twentieth anniversary of the historic Earth Summit. The UN Conference on Sustainable Development, commonly referred to as Rio+20, had two themes—how to build a green economy in the context of sustainable development and poverty eradication, and how to create an international institutional framework for sustainable development. One of the goals of the conference was to secure political commitment for sustainable development, a goal that was advanced as more than $513 billion was pledged by nations at the conference.

One of the main outcomes of the Rio+20 conference was the agreement to create an intergovernmental open working group with the mandate to develop a set of Sustainable Development Goals (SDGs) that would build upon and replace the Millennium Development Goals set to expire in 2015.

While the United Nations has taken a leading role in advancing the agenda for sustainable development, many aspects of the agenda are controversial. *Opposing Viewpoints: Global Sustainability* presents arguments by scientists, journalists, and commentators that provide varying opinions on the issues surrounding global sustainability in chapters titled "Do Genetically Modified Foods Contribute to Global Sustainability?," "Is Water Scarcity a Threat to Global Sustainability?," "Does Social Equity Promote Global Sustainability?," and "Is Economic Growth Compatible with Sustainability?"

CHAPTER 1

Do Genetically Modified Foods Contribute to Global Sustainability?

Chapter Preface

The general public and scientists are widely divided on the safety of eating genetically modified (GM) foods, according to a survey released in January 2015 by the Pew Research Center. While 88 percent of scientists connected with the American Association for the Advancement of Science say GM foods are generally safe, 57 percent of the American public believes GM foods to be unsafe. The center gave as a possible reason for the gap the survey's finding that 67 percent of the public says scientists do not have a clear understanding of the health effects of GM foods.

The release of the survey results set off a flurry of commentary on the potential reasons why the public and scientists are so divided on the issue of genetically modified foods. Writing for the *Washington Post*, Mark Lynas put the blame on the activism of such special interest groups as Greenpeace and the Center for Food Safety, stating "such discrepancies do not happen by accident. In most cases, there are determined lobbies working to undermine public understanding of science."

A fear of the unknown is one reason why the public distrusts genetically modified organisms (GMOs), writes Christie Wilcox at the *Science Sushi* blog. Most people do not understand the complexities of genetic engineering and are distrustful of things they do not understand, she posits. A further factor is the way in which people assess risk, she states, explaining that people weigh risks twice as strongly as gains, a phenomenon called loss aversion. Wilcox states that "the way humans assess risk, saying GM crops will improve yields doesn't feel like a strong reason to support them, but even the slightest chance they could cause disease is more than enough reason to fear them."

The Internet provides a forum for critics of genetically modified foods to state their position, giving nonscientists a platform they did not have in the pre-Internet days, points out Joel Achenbach in *National Geographic*. According to Achenbach, "Gone are the days when a small number of powerful institutions—elite universities, encyclopedias, major news organizations, even *National Geographic*—served as gatekeepers of scientific information. The Internet has democratized information, which is a good thing. But along with cable TV, it has made it possible to live in a 'filter bubble' that lets in only the information with which you already agree."

Writing in 2013 in the *New Yorker*, Maria Konnikova cites psychologist Paul Slovic, who postulates that there are three factors getting in the way of a logical assessment of the risk associated with new technologies: the level of dread, degree of familiarity, and number of people the new technology will affect. According to Konnikova, "GMOs are at the extreme of that scale, high in dread and possible impact, while being low in familiarity." Additionally, Konnikova points out, most people are distrustful of the large corporations that produce GM foods.

In the following chapter, scientists, journalists, and researchers debate the issues surrounding genetically modified foods, including their potential to end world hunger and their safety.

> "It would make a lot more sense to evaluate all crops and all farming practices based on whether they are sustainable, not on the process of developing the seed."

Can GMOs Help Feed a Hot and Hungry World?

Madeline Ostrander

Madeline Ostrander, the former senior editor of Yes! *magazine, is a Seattle-based journalist. In the following viewpoint, Ostrander argues that widespread public distrust of the giant agribusiness Monsanto has made people suspicious of all companies producing genetically engineered crops. Research to create crops that can withstand drought conditions is hampered by a flawed regulatory process and opposition from environmental groups and organic farmers, she reports. The solution to world hunger is to couple genetic engineering with good soil management and other sustainable farming practices, Ostrander concludes.*

As you read, consider the following questions:

1. What are some of the reasons why environmental organizations are suspicious of Monsanto, according to Ostrander?

2. What are some of the potential benefits as well as potential risks to the herbicide Roundup Ready, according to the viewpoint?

3. Why is soil management an important weapon in dealing with drought, according to the organization CalCAN?

Eduardo Blumwald's genetically modified plants don't look much like "Frankenfood." Filling four modest greenhouses in a concrete lot behind Blumwald's laboratory at the University of California [UC], Davis, the tiny seedlings, spiky grasses, alfalfa, and peanut and rice plants in plastic terracotta-colored pots look exactly like the ordinary varieties from which he and his fellow researchers created them. Blumwald's lab lies just ten miles from Monsanto's 90,000-square-foot vegetable seed building, a glassy edifice larger than the hangar for a 747. The Monsanto facility is one of the largest centers in the world for plant breeding and genetic engineering. But in the fourteen years that Blumwald, a professor of cell biology, has worked here studying the DNA [deoxyribonucleic acid] of crop plants he has hardly ever spoken to anyone from Monsanto.

Misguided Activists Stifle Needed Research

Blue-eyed and round-faced, with a lilting Argentinian accent, Blumwald grows exasperated when he talks about the so-called "Big Ag" companies, which he says have been arrogant in dealing with the public, contributing to a distrust of biotech research. But he also doesn't appreciate the activists who've been challenging not only the Monsantos of the world but the entire field of genetic engineering.

"You want to penalize the multinationals; I have no problem with that," he tells me in his office at the university's plant biology building. "But because of your political stance against multinationals, you are going to condemn maybe the only viable solution we have for our future? It's wrong—absolutely wrong."

Blumwald means the hot future that we expect by 2050—when a world population of 9.5 billion people will scramble to put food on the table, while at least thirty-seven separate countries face extreme water crises. Blumwald thinks that part of the answer is to genetically engineer crops that can better withstand drought, and so he and his researchers are scouring the world for varieties of fruits, vegetables and some basic staples—rice, millet, wheat, maize—that grow well without much water. Then, using a device called a "gene gun," which inserts DNA on microscopic gold particles, or a soil bacterium capable of changing plant genes, they alter or silence parts of the plant's genome, adjusting how and when the plant makes the hormones that let it know when to grow and when to wither. The researchers say the methods are more precise and much faster than developing new plant varieties by conventional breeding, which can take decades.

When I tour the rows of rice and peanuts with one of Blumwald's assistants, a postdoctoral researcher from Madrid, the air in the greenhouse is soupy. About two dozen researchers work in Blumwald's lab, many of them from hot parts of the world with swelling populations, including Brazil, China and the United Arab Emirates. In the greenhouse, the researchers force the rice to cope with heat and deprive it of water just as it's about to set seed. So far, the genetically altered rice is outperforming the natural kind—given less moisture, the non-engineered rice browns and wilts, but the new plant survives. Blumwald's goal is to create crops that won't keel over as quickly when things get hot, dry and stressful—plants that will improve the odds that a farmer can produce food even in a drought.

In about forty years, relentless dry spells may be more frequent across the Southwest, say climate scientists, and California may have more dry years like this one [2014], in which a drought has crippled the agricultural sector. But the state, one of the most fiercely contested battlegrounds in a worldwide fight over the use of genetically modified organisms (GMOs), isn't the most inviting home for research like Blumwald's. Since the 1980s, activists here have run a series of campaigns to require the labeling of GM products and an outright ban on GMO cultivation. Blumwald says the controversy over GMOs has made it more difficult to pursue his research and obtain funding. And even if his GM plants could be an important part of the solution to climate change, they may never make their way into the hands of commercial farmers. Who will invest in his plants, test them in the field and market them if they attract boycotts, protests and lawsuits that make business difficult and consumers skittish?

Many biotech researchers and agronomists argue that a combination of bad will generated by Big Ag and misdirected public outrage is stifling important technological advances in agriculture—innovations that could help prevent famine, fight crop diseases and cope with climate change. But countless activists disagree. The Organic Consumers Association, a nonprofit agricultural watchdog group, says genetic engineering will never deliver on promises to feed a growing population and isn't a trustworthy technology. "The dirty secret of the biotech industry is, after thirty years, they haven't done anything for consumers," said Andrew Kimbrell, the founder and executive director of the Center for Food Safety, in a speech at a national heirloom-seed fair in Santa Rosa, California. "No better taste, no more nutrition, zero benefits," and a number of "potential risks."

Monsanto's History with Pesticides Creates Distrust

Over the past several years, the political fight over GMOs has become supercharged, and much of the controversy has been driven by a distrust of big business—and of any of the novel biotechnologies it might produce.

"The same corporations that brought us DDT [dichlorodiphenyltrichloroethane] and Agent Orange now want to deny us our right to know what's in our food," argued California Right to Know during a 2012 campaign that brought together a coalition of organic farmers, environmental organizations, grassroots groups like MOMS Advocating Sustainability, and companies like Clif Bar and Dr. Bronner's Magic Soaps. Two years ago, this coalition attempted to pass a statewide referendum that would have required the labeling of food containing GMOs. The anti-GMO activists were vastly outspent: Monsanto alone invested $8 million in efforts to defeat the measure. But the pro-labeling campaign helped launch a movement. This year alone, a series of similar initiatives have been proposed in twenty states, according to the Center for Food Safety; this past April, Vermont became the first state to pass a GMO labeling law. The Grocery Manufacturers Association and several other trade groups have filed a lawsuit to overturn it.

The California campaign's messages were a jab at Monsanto, in part. Since the 1940s, the company has been manufacturing and selling chemicals, including DDT, the now banned herbicide that contributed to the near extinction of bald eagles in the twentieth century. In the 1960s, the company distributed a brochure mocking Rachel Carson's seminal work, *Silent Spring*, the book that first brought widespread public attention to the dangers of pesticides and launched the modern environmental movement. Around the same time, Monsanto was producing Agent Orange, the chemical weapon used to strip vegetation in Vietnam war zones—and later linked to birth defects and cancers there and in the United States.

In 1997, Monsanto partly reinvented itself, transferring most of its chemical business to a company called Pharmacia, which later became part of Pfizer. Today, the only chemicals that Monsanto produces are agricultural, including Roundup, an herbicide that the company invented in 1970. It has marketed genetically modified seed since the 1990s; its premier products, among the most common GM crops on the market, are "Roundup Ready"—varieties of soybeans, corn, alfalfa, cotton, canola and sugar beets whose DNAs have been modified to keep them from dying when doused with Roundup. In the big grain-growing regions of the United States, such as the Midwest, Roundup Ready is the industry standard. As a result, Roundup, which also goes by the chemical name glyphosate, is the most commonly used herbicide in the country.

Because the DNA of Monsanto's GM plants is patented, the company has enormous control over the US food system. It has brought 145 suits against American farmers for patent infringement—i.e., for intentionally or, according to at least one farmer, accidentally (since grain DNA travels along with pollen in the wind) growing Monsanto's GM varieties without paying for them.

The explosion of the Roundup Ready market may have environmental upsides. One biotech researcher I spoke with noted that the use of Roundup Ready seed has reduced reliance on even more toxic agricultural chemicals, and US Department of Agriculture data concur. Roundup is considered more benign than many herbicides: It tends not to linger in the soil and is sometimes used even in places like nature preserves to beat back aggressive weeds. But few chemicals intended to poison plants or pests are entirely harm free, and new research indicates that Roundup could be more damaging than previously thought: It may contribute to miscarriages and interfere with fetal development. And around the country, weeds that are resistant to Roundup are proliferating. Dow AgroSciences, a division of Dow Chemical and another major player in agribusiness, is about to release a new generation of genetically modified crops that tolerate a more powerful and persistent herbicide—2,4-D [dichlorophenoxyacetic acid], a potential neurotoxin.

According to Robert Fraley, Monsanto's chief technology officer and executive vice president, his company has been studying the impacts of climate change since 2006. But it has created only one line of GM plants designed to deal with environmental stress—a type of corn called DroughtGard. Like Blumwald's plants, DroughtGard doesn't die back as quickly when the weather is dry, though the mechanism driving this trait is different: It relies on inserting bacterial DNA into the plant. In field trials in the Great Plains, DroughtGard performed modestly better than other varieties of corn. Monsanto has now made it available commercially to farmers, and China has approved the seed for import.

But even if such technologies prove useful in mitigating the impacts of climate change, Monsanto's tarnished history, heavy-handed dealings with the public, lawsuits, and sheer size and might have made it a favorite villain. To a certain segment of the public, everything that Monsanto does is suspect, and genetic engineering looks like a strategy for pushing the company's brand of herbicides and manipulating the food economy—not a way to a feed a world in crisis.

Genetically Modified Food Dates Back to 1982

It can be easy to forget that genetic engineering has an existence and a history beyond Big Ag. Monsanto's website credits Robert Fraley, then a researcher for the company, with producing the first GM plant in 1982, but there were at least three other institutions working simultaneously—two universities in the United States and one in Belgium—to grow the first plants with spliced genes that year. In the decades since, scores of university researchers, small research and development ventures and even a few nonprofits have used genetic engineering to try to stop diseases from decimating citrus plants, create mustard plants that can clean up toxins from mining and industrial sites, and grow food that can better survive in heat, drought, flooding, freezing and other extreme weather conditions that may get worse in the next several decades.

But almost none of these plants have ever made it beyond a field-testing stage. As of 2010, though 260 genetically engineered traits have been tested in seventy-seven different "specialty crops" (foods that are less profitable and produced on a smaller scale than field corn, cotton, soy, wheat and rice), just four varieties—including insecticide-resistant sweet corn, disease-resistant papaya and squash, and an ornamental purple carnation—are on the market, according to a review by Jamie Miller and Kent Bradford, researchers with the Seed Biotechnology Center at UC Davis. That's nothing near the scope of innovation one would need to confront a problem as vast as climate change or famine.

When I spoke with Bradford, he blamed anti-GMO activists, in part, for making R&D [research and development] difficult: "Those groups have driven all of the biotechnology work into the companies they hate," he said. "They've made it impossible for anybody else by raising a stink. Even if the regulatory bars don't seem so high, [activist groups] will sue." Only big companies like Monsanto can afford the legal and regulatory costs to test GM varieties and bring them to market, Bradford argues.

Current Regulatory Process Is Not Working

Neither biotech researchers nor GMO opponents think the current regulatory process is working well. Anti-GMO groups insist that the Food and Drug Administration's [FDA's] approval process is too opaque and leaves GMO testing in the hands of food companies. Biotech researchers counter that, in practice, the FDA insists on exhaustive and expensive testing far beyond what has been required for any other kind of food crop, even though years of research suggest that the technology of genetic engineering is safe. The American Association for the Advancement of Science, for example, has announced that "foods containing ingredients from [GM] crops pose no greater risk than the same foods made from crops modified by conventional plant breeding." Bradford and others insist that it doesn't make scientific sense to single out GM crops for special testing when other, far less precise methods of crop development—including blasting plants with radiation—aren't subject to such rigorous scrutiny.

The high cost of GMO field-testing may explain why the only genetically modified crops that have made it to market are, in the words of environmental scientist Jonathan Foley, "very disappointing" and "come with some big problems."

"GMO efforts may have started off with good intentions to improve food security," Foley wrote in a column in the science magazine Ensia in February, "but they ended up in crops that were better at improving profits."

Organic Farmers Oppose GMOs

Whether Blumwald's plants—or the hundreds of other GM crops designed to be disease or climate change resistant or otherwise useful in feeding the world—ever make it to farm fields may depend a lot on whether food activists, the public and policy makers can be persuaded that the technology is able to produce worthwhile results.

The heart of one GMO battle is roughly fifty miles west of Blumwald's lab, in Sonoma County—a land of wineries, towering redwood groves poised at the edge of rocky coastal cliffs, and some of the most innovative organic agriculture in the country.

Much of the opposition to GMOs here has come from organic farmers, partly out of fear that their crops will be tainted by cross-pollination by GM varieties. Under organic certification rules, farmers aren't allowed to grow GMOs, and their customers often refuse to eat GM food. In March 2004, Mendocino County, just north of Sonoma, became the first jurisdiction in the nation to pass a law regulating GM plants, making it illegal to "propagate, cultivate, raise, or grow" them, in order to stop what it called "genetic pollution"; Marin County, to the south, passed a similar ordinance the following November. A grassroots group in Sonoma County is now actively pushing for a countywide ban on GMOs.

Here, on a plot of forest in the tiny unincorporated town of Occidental, several longtime environmental activists run a center for sustainable agriculture research in a cluster of yurts and wood cabins that form an intentional community called the Occidental Arts and Ecology Center (OAEC). Its leader, Dave Henson, cofounded Californians for GE-Free Agriculture, a coalition that ran campaigns against GMOs between 2002 and 2008. But when I asked him how he felt about genetic engineering, his answer surprised me. "If this is public research at a university, I think we will see some really interesting potential solutions with recombinant DNA that could show all kinds of benefits in health and agriculture and other things," he said. "So baby and bathwater are separate." Henson added that he's even guest lectured to classrooms of biotechnology graduate students at UC Berkeley.

A Systemic Solution Is Needed

When I described Blumwald's research, however, Henson was skeptical. "The biotech solution is to change out one variety of one crop with another single variety that's somehow more adapted by genetic engineering," he said, while the approach to climate change, drought and other related issues "should be about the whole farm system."

And that's the major area of disagreement between food activists and the farm industry: People like Henson believe the entire system of modern agriculture needs a radical makeover to rely less on fossil fuels, irrigation, and the chemical fertilizers and weed killers that are fouling water sources from the Great Lakes to the Mississippi [River]. Tweaking a gene won't fix all that, Henson argues: "The solution has got to be a return to a more sustainable, soil-focused agriculture."

Five years ago, Henson, OAEC, and several other groups and individuals involved with the GE-free coalition partnered with organic and family farmers to form a new organization, the California Climate and Agriculture Network (CalCAN). Their intent was to involve farmers in California's new climate change law, the most comprehensive policy on global warming in the country. At the time, the group was also responding to Monsanto. "It was informed by the advertising campaign that Monsanto was doing . . . around its development of GMO crops that they claimed would respond to a number of [environmental] issues," says Renata Brillinger, who now heads the group. In 2008 and 2009, Monsanto placed ads in publications like the *New Yorker* and the *Atlantic* and on the radio program *Marketplace* arguing that its biotech seeds would be necessary to feed the world's burgeoning population. "We saw a need for other solutions," Brillinger adds.

Today, CalCAN has no formal position on GMOs, but simply says that it wants, in Brillinger's words, "shovel-ready" solutions to deal with the drought right now. Most of these are about managing soil. Rich, organic soil—the kind that can be developed by using manure and compost more and tilling less—holds water better than poor soil. In a drought, plants grown in rich soil are less thirsty; in a deluge, such soil absorbs and slows the flow of water, thereby decreasing flooding and erosion. Organic matter is also high in carbon, and storing it in the soil keeps it out of the atmosphere, helping to address the problem of climate change itself. CalCAN has focused on statewide policy, including efforts to wring funding from the California budget to promote soil- and water-conservation practices and climate change strategies for farmers. To Brillinger, GMO research looks costly and difficult; managing the soil is immediate, cheap and much easier.

Genetically Modified Crops Are Part of the Solution

Down the road, in Sebastopol, I found a small organic farm that made this convincing. Paul Kaiser drove up to meet me in front of his barn in a small green tractor, then walked me through the densely planted rows spanning his two acres of crop fields, filled with roughly 150 varieties of vegetables. "We earn over $100,000 per crop acre per year," he says. (By contrast, the average revenue from an acre of California cabbages or cucumbers in 2012 was about $6,000 to $8,000, according to the state's Department of Food and Agriculture.) Kaiser credits his soil-management practices for his financial success.

Before farming, he worked in agroforestry, restoring fields in the tropics that were so overgrazed they could barely grow grass. To Kaiser, the question of engineering any single plant is unimportant compared with a larger picture involving soil, water, bees, and the various other insects and birds that can thrive on an organic farm and provide natural pest control. Kaiser supports the ban in Sonoma County: "Unless we can prove that a GMO crop is fully safe and beneficial to everything that it touches—the pollinators, the soil it's grown in, the watershed and our body—we shouldn't be using it," he says.

At its core, nothing about the science of gene splicing precludes good soil management and other sustainable practices. Pamela Ronald, a UC Davis plant pathology professor, and her husband Raoul Adamchak, a farmer and former board president of the group California Certified Organic Farmers, insist that it's not only possible but necessary to combine techniques like soil conservation with genetic engineering. They've also written a book on the subject called *Tomorrow's Table*.

Ronald argues that those who object to GMOs are focused on the wrong questions: "It would make a lot more sense to evaluate all crops and all farming practices based on whether they are sustainable, not on the process of developing the seed. We know that the process itself is no more risky than any other kind of genetic process." GM crops will never be a silver bullet, she adds, and we can't confront a food crisis without also dealing with the other shortcomings of large-scale agriculture. Even so, genetic modification does offer help, and in a crisis, even a small fix can be worth a lot. Ronald and her colleague, David Mackill, used a combination of genetic engineering and plant breeding to create a variety of rice that can withstand the flooding that has inundated much of Bangladesh and India and devastated the rice fields, a disaster made worse by climate change. Last year, the rice was grown by 4 million farmers.

Ronald doesn't point fingers at any one party for the public relations difficulties faced by biotech researchers. But she does note that the solution to a world food crisis won't emerge only in the lab: "There seems to be a communication gap between organic and conventional farmers, as well as between consumers and scientists. It is time to close that gap," she and Adamchak conclude in *Tomorrow's Table*. "Science and good farming alone will not be sufficient."

"*Despite the PR, Monsanto's goal is not to make hunger history. It's to control the staple crops that feed the world.*"

Genetically Modified Foods Are Not the Answer to World Hunger

John Robbins

John Robbins is the founder of EarthSave as well as the co-founder and president of the Food Revolution Network. He is the author of nine books, including Diet for a New America. *In July 2000,* Time *magazine ran a story called "Grains of Hope" that heralded golden rice, a genetically modified crop, as proof that agricultural biotechnology can successfully address world hunger. The promise of golden rice has not been fulfilled, according to Robbins in the following viewpoint. It is expensive to grow because it requires large amounts of fertilizers, pesticides, and water, he claims. Robbins argues the real motivation of Monsanto and other businesses creating genetically modified organisms is not to solve world hunger; it is to enhance their profits.*

As you read, consider the following questions:

1. What are some of the issues with golden rice, according to Robbins?

2. Why do some people still go hungry, according to George Monbiot?

3. According to the viewpoint, why do critics refer to genetically engineered seeds as "suicide seeds"?

Can genetically engineered foods help feed the hungry? Are anti-GMO [genetically modified organism] activists and overzealous environmentalists standing in the way of the hungry being fed?

Biotech Companies Spent Millions Promoting GMOs

The hope that GMO foods might bring solutions to malnutrition and world hunger was never more dramatically illustrated than when *Time* magazine ran a cover story titled "Grains of Hope." The article joyfully announced the development of a genetically engineered "golden rice." This new strain of GM [genetically modified] rice has genes from viruses and daffodils spliced into its genetic instructions. The result is a form of rice that is a golden-yellow color (much like daffodil flowers), and that produces beta-carotene, which the human body normally converts into vitamin A.

Nearly a million children die every year because they are weakened by vitamin A deficiencies and an additional 350,000 go blind. Golden rice, said *Time*, will be a godsend for the half of humanity that depends on rice for its major staple. Merely eating this rice could prevent blindness and death.

The development of golden rice was, it seemed, compelling and inspiring evidence that GM crops could be the answer to malnutrition and hunger. *Time* quoted former U.S. president Jimmy Carter: "Responsible biotechnology is not the enemy, starvation is."

Shortly after the *Time* cover story, Monsanto and other biotechnology companies launched a $50 million marketing campaign, including $32 million in TV and print advertising. The ads, complete with soft-focus fields and smiling children, said that "biotech foods could help end world hunger."

Other ad campaigns have followed. One Monsanto ad tells the public: "Biotechnology is one of tomorrow's tools in our hands today. Slowing its acceptance is a luxury our hungry world cannot afford."

Within a few months, the biotech industry had spent far more on these ads than it had on developing golden rice. Their purpose? "Unless I'm missing something," wrote Michael Pollan in the *New York Times Magazine*, "the aim of this audacious new advertising campaign is to impale people like me—well-off first-worlders dubious about genetically engineered food—on the horns of a moral dilemma. . . . If we don't get over our queasiness about eating genetically modified food, kids in the third world will go blind."

If you believe the ads, you'd think that lifesaving food is being held hostage by anti-science activists.

In the years since *Time* proclaimed the promises of golden rice, however, we've learned a few things.

The Early Promise of Golden Rice Was Erroneous

For one thing, we've learned that golden rice will not grow in the kinds of soil that it must to be of value to the world's hungry. To grow properly, it requires heavy use of fertilizers and pesticides—expensive inputs unaffordable to the very people that the variety is supposed to help. And we've also learned that golden rice requires large amounts of water—water that might not be available in precisely those areas where vitamin A deficiency is a problem, and where farmers cannot afford costly irrigation projects.

And one more thing—it turns out that golden rice doesn't work, even in theory. Malnourished people are not able to absorb vitamin A in this form. And even if they could, they'd have to eat an awful lot of the stuff. An 11-year-old boy would have to eat 27 bowls of golden rice a day in order to satisfy his minimum requirement for the vitamin.

I'm sure that given enough time and enough money, some viable genetically modified (GM) crops could be developed that contain more nutrients or have higher yields. But I'm not sure that even if that were to happen, it would actually benefit the world's poor. Monsanto and the other biotech companies aren't developing these seeds with the intention of giving them away. If people can't afford to buy GM seeds, or if they can't afford the fertilizers, pesticides and water the seeds require, they'll be left out.

Profit Is the Goal of Biotech Companies

Poverty is at the root of the problem of hunger. As Peter Rosset, director of Food First, reminds us, "People do not have vitamin A deficiency because rice contains too little vitamin A, but because their diet has been reduced to rice and almost nothing else."

And what, pray tell, has reduced these people to such poverty and their diets to such meager fare? In the words of the British writer George Monbiot:

> "The world has a surplus of food, but still people go hungry. They go hungry because they cannot afford to buy it. They cannot afford to buy it because the sources of wealth and the means of production have been captured and in some cases monopolized by landowners and corporations. The purpose of the biotech industry is to capture and monopolize the sources of wealth and the means of production. . . .

GMO Crops Are Not the Answer

By the end of the century, the world may well have to accommodate ten billion inhabitants—roughly the equivalent of adding two new Indias. Sustaining that many people will require farmers to grow more food in the next seventy-five years than has been produced in all of human history. For most of the past ten thousand years, feeding more people simply meant farming more land. That option no longer exists; nearly every arable patch of ground has been cultivated, and irrigation for agriculture already consumes seventy per cent of Earth's freshwater.

The nutritional demands of the developing world's rapidly growing middle class—more protein from pork, beef, chicken, and eggs—will add to the pressure; so will the ecological impact of climate change, particularly in India and other countries where farmers depend on monsoons. Many scientists are convinced that we can hope to meet those demands only with help from the advanced tools of plant genetics. . . .

Genetically modified crops will not solve the problem of the hundreds of millions of people who go to bed hungry every night. It would be far better if the world's foods contained an adequate supply of vitamins. . . . No single crop or approach to farming can possibly feed the world. To prevent billions of people from living in hunger, we will need to use every one of them.

Michael Specter, "Seeds of Doubt,"
New Yorker, *August 25, 2014.*

GM technology permits companies to ensure that everything we eat is owned by them. They can patent the seeds and the processes which give rise to them. They can make sure that crops can't be grown without their patented chemicals. They can prevent seeds from reproducing themselves. By buying up competing seed companies and closing them down, they can capture the food market, the biggest and most diverse market of all.

No one in her right mind would welcome this, so the corporations must persuade us to focus on something else. . . . We are told that . . . by refusing to eat GM products, we are threatening the developing world with starvation, an argument that is, shall we say, imaginative. . . ."

The biotech companies have invested billions of dollars because they sense in this technology the potential for enormous profit and the means to gain control over the world's food supply. Their goal is not to help subsistence farmers feed themselves. Their goal is to maximum profit.

While Monsanto would like us to believe it is seeking to alleviate world hunger, there is actually a very dark side to the company's efforts. For countless centuries, farmers have fed humanity by saving the seed from one year's crop to plant the following year. But Monsanto, the company that claims its motives are to help feed the hungry, has developed what it calls a "Technology Protection System" that renders seeds sterile. Commonly known as "terminator technology" and developed with taxpayer funding by the USDA [US Department of Agriculture] and Delta & Pine Land Company (an affiliate of Monsanto), the process genetically alters seeds so that their offspring will be sterile for all time. If employed, this technology would ensure that farmers cannot save their own seeds, but would have to come back to Monsanto year after year to purchase new ones.

Critics refer to these genetically engineered seeds as suicide seeds. "By peddling suicide seeds, the biotechnology multinationals will lock the world's poorest farmers into a new form of genetic serfdom," says Emma Must of the World Development Movement [presently known as Global Justice

Now]. "Currently 80 percent of crops in developing countries are grown using farm-saved seed. Being unable to save seeds from sterile crops could mean the difference between surviving and going under."

To Monsanto and other GMO companies, the terminator and other seed sterilizing technologies are simply business ventures that are designed to enhance profits. In this case, there is not even the implication of benefit to consumers.

I wish I could speak more highly of GM foods and their potential. But the technology is now held tightly in the hands of corporations whose motives are, I'm afraid, very different from what they would have us believe.

Despite the PR, Monsanto's goal is not to make hunger history. It's to control the staple crops that feed the world.

Will GMOs help end world hunger? I don't think so.

| "Through advanced research and new farming methods, hunger can be fought and conquered."

Genetically Modified Foods Can Help Address the Global Food Crisis

David Weisser

David Weisser is a research associate with the National Center for Policy Analysis. With the world projected to add 2.3 billion people from 2009 to 2050, it will need to increase food production by 70 percent, maintains Weisser in the following viewpoint. This scale of increase is not achievable by conventional farming methods and requires the development of genetically modified organisms to increase crop yields, he claims. Weisser cites the successes of biotech cotton in India, biotech sugarcane in Brazil, and biotech corn in the United States as proof that genetically modified foods can help address world hunger.

David Weisser, "The Future of Farming and Rise of Biotechnology," National Center for Policy Analysis, Issue Brief, no. 152, October 21, 2014. Copyright © 2014 by National Center for Policy Analysis. All rights reserved. Reproduced with permission.

As you read, consider the following questions:

1. According to the viewpoint, what was the world's population in 2009, and what is it projected to grow to by 2050?

2. How does biotechnology improve the characteristics of food crops, according to Weisser?

3. In the study of Indian cotton farms cited by Weisser, what were the impacts on yield and cost by adopting biotech cotton?

Today, more than 800 million people are malnourished, meaning they do not get the minimum energy requirements set by the United Nations [U.N] Food and Agriculture Organization (FAO) of 1,690 calories per day for an urban adult and 1,650 calories for a rural dweller.

The world's population is projected to grow by 2.3 billion people from 2009 to 2050, to 9.1 billion. To feed that many people adequately will require a 70 percent increase in food production globally and a doubling of food production in developing countries.

There are natural limits to the productivity increases that can be obtained with conventional farming. Scientifically advanced biotechnology could greatly benefit the world's growing population, but governments have placed severe regulatory restrictions on the use of such technology. The most controversial aspect of biotechnology is the development of genetically modified organisms (GMOs) to increase crop yields per acre and to improve the nutritional quality of the food produced. Restrictions on the development and cultivation of biotech crops have slowed global progress in conquering hunger. Through advanced research and new farming methods, global hunger could be reduced.

The Problem of Global Hunger

Every year, U.N. agencies gather to discuss the continuing hunger crisis. By utilizing existing programs, the U.N. hopes to achieve a lasting balance between the food supply and the nutritional demands of a growing population, but the plans proposed to achieve this balance vary widely. Furthermore, there is a persistent drive to increase conventional farming rather than to utilize biotechnology.

Essentially, biotechnology improves the characteristics and requirements of food crops through manipulation of plant DNA [deoxyribonucleic acid], or genetic engineering, creating a GMO. Such plants have better insect resistance and herbicide tolerance, and the sustainability of cultivation is increased by minimizing use of pesticides and fertilizers. A common way this is done is by introducing genes from the *Bacillus thuringiensis* (Bt) bacterium. Though additional productivity increases could be achieved through conventional farming, such as more widespread use of chemical fertilizers, biotechnology is essential. Rather than discourage the growth of biotech crops, the U.N. should promote their development and use.

Multinational organizations, such as the European Union [EU], should ease restrictions on the importation, planting and sale of GMOs. On June 12, 2014, the European Council moved to allow member states to restrict or ban the cultivation of EU-authorized GMOs within their own territory. No GMO can be cultivated within the EU without prior authorization and risk assessment from national evaluation agencies, the European Food Safety Authority and approval from the member state in which it will be cultivated.

It has been claimed that biotech crops are more expensive than conventional crops and do not improve yields, but evidence from around the globe shows the opposite is true.

Biotech Cotton in India

As India's population has continued to increase beyond the number that can be fed by traditional agriculture, the adoption of biotech crops has grown. A study conducted from 2002–2008 sought to determine the yield advantages of biotechnology crops. Of 533 cotton farms examined in the study, 38 percent had adopted Bollgard Bt cotton in 2002, a strain of Bt cotton developed by Monsanto, a major biotechnology company. By the end of the study in 2008, 99 percent of the sample households had adopted Bt cotton.

Bt cotton is able to ward off insects and pests without additional pesticides. Reducing the need for pesticides minimizes environmental damage while increasing agricultural yields. Initially, 290,000 hectares were planted with Bt cotton. By 2012, that number had reached 9.4 million hectares. (A hectare is equivalent to a little more than 2 acres.)

To calculate yields, scientists conducted a survey of how much is grown in a sample area. On one cotton farm, the yield increased 7,625.7 pounds per hectare while reducing the costs by $143.32 per hectare through less use of pesticides. This increase in production is raising the incomes of cotton farmers and farm laborers, and it is allowing many farmers to invest in upgrading their machinery. The majority of small independent cotton farmers in India rely on cotton as a cash crop, and they buy food locally with the revenue earned from their crops. Thus, Bt cotton has not only increased yields beyond the capability of conventional farming, it has also created a more technologically advanced agricultural economy in India.

Biotech Sugarcane in Brazil

Brazil produces roughly 588 million tons of sugarcane per year, nearly half of the world's output. It has the potential to double the amount produced to roughly 1.176 billion tons. However, it is estimated that Brazilians lose more than half of their potential yield to drought, pests and weeds. These losses have encouraged the widespread adoption of biotechnology in Brazil.

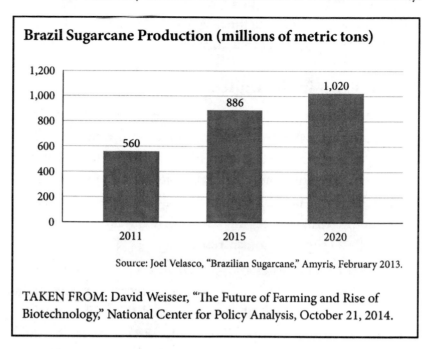

Brazil Sugarcane Production (millions of metric tons)

Source: Joel Velasco, "Brazilian Sugarcane," Amyris, February 2013.

TAKEN FROM: David Weisser, "The Future of Farming and Rise of Biotechnology," National Center for Policy Analysis, October 21, 2014.

Brazil is the world's number two producer of genetically modified crops, after the United States. As with corn in the United States, sugarcane in Brazil is used as food as well as an energy source. Transportation biofuels are so cheap in Brazil that sugarcane ethanol is downgrading gasoline to an alternative fuel. As the world's population increases, so does the need for energy.

The move to biotechnology crops in Brazil began in the early 1990s when researchers began experimenting with soybeans due to their widespread use. However, until March 2003, a government ban prevented the use of GMOs. Lifting the ban has allowed Monsanto, which spends $1.5 billion annually on research worldwide, to conduct biotechnology research in Brazil.

In 2009, Brazil created and approved for use a new strain of sugarcane projected to increase average annual yields by 20 tons per hectare. By 2020, annual projected demand for sugar will increase 13.7 million tons. With biotechnology, Brazil is getting closer to meeting that demand.

Biotech Corn in the United States

While countries around the world are slowly gaining access to biotech crops, the United States has revolutionized the industry. One of the most well-known biotech crops in the world is corn. Corn, like sugarcane, has multiple uses. Many countries around the world use it for ethanol, food and even bioplastics. With such a wide variety of uses, corn quickly became the most desired crop for biotech research.

More than any other crop, corn has significant research potential. In the United States, there are several varieties of Bt corn that have been genetically engineered to resist herbicides and pests and even withstand drought. Further research could include salinity immunity, which would allow corn and other crops to be planted in soil which would otherwise be unable to sustain agricultural life. These advances are especially useful in developing countries seeking locally sustainable farming.

Nearly 20 percent of all U.S. corn and 50 percent of all U.S. soybeans are exported to other nations, yet it is still not enough to feed the world population. Furthermore, there are many regions in the world in addition to the European Union that do not allow the production or importation of biotech crops, greatly reducing both the amount of food and technology that can be transferred internationally.

Meanwhile, 88 percent of corn grown in the United States has been altered utilizing biotechnology. This has propelled production to numbers never thought possible, allowing the United States to remain the global leader in corn production. But the world economy is currently unable to take full advantage of biotechnology. With decreased regulation, however, the ability to feed the world would be easily attainable.

GMOs Can Help Conquer Global Hunger

Global hunger will only continue to increase and combating it will not be easy, yet the world is fortunate in that a wealth of research is dedicated to the advancement of farming. For instance, Nobel Prize winner Norman Borlaug was recognized for surpassing technological limits and pushed the boundaries of conventional farming through the use of biotechnology. Borlaug did so by breeding crops with desirable characteristics in an era when it was not possible to directly manipulate DNA. His research alone is credited for saving nearly a billion lives, and he was applauded by President Barack Obama for his dedication to feeding the world.

Placing limits on biotechnology restricts the advancements that Borlaug pioneered and only hurts the world's starving population. Interest groups will continue to combat the use and production of GMOs, but science will continue to dominate the industry. Through advanced research and new farming methods, hunger can be fought and conquered.

"So really, the question isn't how will we feed 9 billion by 2050? The question is, how many people will we really have and what will they be eating?"

Genetically Modified Foods Will Not Help Address the Global Food Crisis

Samuel Fromartz

Samuel Fromartz is editor in chief of the Food & Environment Reporting Network, a nonprofit journalism organization. He is also the author of In Search of the Perfect Loaf: A Home Baker's Odyssey *and* Organic, Inc.: Natural Foods and How They Grew. *In the following viewpoint, Fromartz argues that the reasoning that genetically modified crops are needed to provide food for a worldwide population that is expected to swell by two billion by 2050 is based on a faulty premise. He quotes economist Douglas Southgate, who suggests a much lower growth rate in population is likely. Also of importance are food choices, Fromartz contends. The solution is not genetically modified crops but rather reducing world poverty and choosing diets that are less resource intensive, he concludes.*

As you read, consider the following questions:

1. How are GMOs making the problem of world hunger worse, according to Fromartz?

2. What are the five menu items of possible food lifestyles, according to the viewpoint?

3. According to the viewpoint, what are the impacts of rising incomes on food consumption?

With food prices hitting record highs, people are rioting and political regimes are crumbling. We can only imagine what it will be like when the global population rises to 9 billion in 2050 from just under 7 billion now. More riots, more deforestation, more hunger, more revolutions? How are these people going to be fed? The unequivocal answer we so often hear: biotechnology.

Population Estimates for 2050 Are Debatable

Let's ignore for the moment the cause of rising food prices, which have been attributed to everything from bad weather and poor harvests to higher oil prices that push up the cost of fertilizers, the rise of biofuels, even commodity index funds (which are bidding up futures, though I'm skeptical they are leading the parade). The thing I get hung up on is the "9 billion." It makes a great sound bite but what's behind the figure?

So far the vast resources of commercial biotechnology have gone to commodity crops such as corn and soybeans (and soon alfalfa). The majority ends up as animal feed, and thus meat, which is the least efficient way to produce calories. Meat also happens to be available to the richest people, not the poorest. So, we haven't really used genetically modified organisms (GMOs) to "feed the world." Instead we've used them to bring down the cost of industrial meat production and incentivize a transition to a meat-centric diet. The loss of calories that results from feeding grains to animals instead of humans represents the annual calorie needs of more than 3.5 billion people, according to the UN [United Nations] Environment Programme. In short, GMOs arguably are making matters worse by fueling the production of more animal feed and food-competing biofuels.

Be that as it may, we're still stuck with the 9 billion problem. Population is like compounding interest, with small changes producing big results down the road. So the growth rate is hugely important and it doesn't always do what's expected. *National Geographic* had an interesting take on this, showing that the argument popular in the 1960s about a "population bomb" largely turned out to be a fiction. By the early 1970s, fertility rates around the world had begun dropping faster than anyone had anticipated. Since then, the population growth rate has fallen by more than 40 percent:

> In industrialized countries it took generations for fertility to fall to the replacement level or below. As that same transition takes place in the rest of the world, what has astonished demographers is how much faster it is happening there. . . .

> "The problem has become a bit passé," Hervé Le Bras (a French demographer) says. Demographers are generally confident that by the second half of this century we will be ending one unique era in history—the population explosion—and entering another, in which population will level out or even fall.

This is why numbers are important. On that score, Andrew Revkin had an interesting exchange on the *Dot Earth* blog at the *[New York] Times* that showed a range of opinions on what it would take to "feed the world." Revkin's post noted that Douglas Southgate, an agricultural economist at Ohio State University, "argues that a low growth scenario for population, leading to just under 8 billion people by 2050, could see a 26 percent drop in food prices even with substantial rise in consumption." This is considered the low range for 2050, but considering how off the mark Malthusians [believers in the theory of Thomas Robert Malthus that posits that population tends to increase at a faster rate than its means of subsistence] were in the past, it shouldn't be entirely discounted.

Food Choices Are a Major Variable

But let's say we do get to 9 billion. The impact on resources, it turns out, depends a lot on what we eat. Vaclav Smil, a University of Manitoba analyst, pointed out to Revkin "a menu of possible food lifestyles," which for a world of 9 billion meant either bountiful supplies or scarcity. Here's the spectrum:

1. Eating enough to survive with reduced life spans (Ethiopia)

2. Eating enough to have some sensible, though limited, choices and to live near full life spans when considering other (hygienic, health care) circumstances (as in the better parts of India today)

3. Having more than enough of overall food energy but still a limited choice of plant foods and only a healthy minimum of animal foods and live close to or just past 70 (China of the late 1980s and 1990s)

4. Not wanting more carbohydrates and shifting more crop production and imports to [livestock] feed, not food, to eat more animal products, having overall some 3,000 kcal/capita a day and living full spans (China now)

5. Having gross surpluses of everything, total supply at 3,500–3,700 kcal/day, eating too much animal protein, wasting 35–40% of all food, living record life spans, getting sick (U.S. and E.U. today)

Obviously, we want to avoid option one and two, as much as possible. Option three and four would mean 1 billion

Risks of GM Crops Outweigh the Benefits

Genetically modified (GM) crops and foods are promoted on the basis of a range of far-reaching claims from the industry and its supporters. . . .

However, a large and growing body of scientific and other authoritative evidence shows that these claims are not true. On the contrary, evidence presented in this report indicates that GM crops:

- Are laboratory made, using technology that is totally different from natural breeding methods, and pose different risks from non-GM crops.
- Can be toxic, allergenic or less nutritious than their natural counterparts.
- Are not adequately regulated to ensure safety.
- Do not increase yield potential.
- Do not reduce pesticide use but increase it. . . .
- Cannot solve the problem of world hunger but distract from its real causes—poverty, lack of access to food and, increasingly, lack of access to land to grow it on. . . .

There is no need to take risks with GM crops when effective, readily available, and sustainable solutions to the problems that GM technology is claimed to address already exist.

John Fagan, Michael Antoniou, and Claire Robinson,
GMO Myths and Truths. *2nd ed.*
London: Earth Open Source, 2014.

people who lack enough food today would be better off. But Smil says, "The world eating between levels 3–4 would not know what to do with today's food." In other words, we have enough already. But, he also adds, "the world at 5 is impossible." Nor is it desirable, considering the obesity crisis and health risks.

So really, the question isn't how will we feed 9 billion by 2050? The question is, how many people will we really have and what will they be eating?

Poverty Is a Major Factor

Poverty of course plays a big role in both these issues because, as Juergen Voegele, director, agriculture and rural development, the World Bank, pointed out to Revkin: "We already have close to one billion people who go hungry today, not because there is not enough food in the world but because they cannot afford to buy it."

Rising incomes, of course, is a difficult nut—one that doesn't succumb to a solution hatched in a lab. But more income means better educated families, and even declining population growth. The flip side, though, is that rising incomes are also associated with higher meat consumption, which can get us closer to option five on Smil's lifestyles if we are not careful. So the best case: to raise incomes *and* to incentivize less resource-intensive food consumption.

But we don't need to become vegans to save the world (which would doom us even if we did because so few would go along). In many developing countries, such an approach would amount to culinary imperialism, given the importance of meat for both income generation, the result of having a cow or goat or two, and as a source of much-needed calories for children from milk and scant meat. Never mind the use of manure to grow crops. We're not talking about factory farms here, but animals that play a central role in cultures and livelihoods.

As the [*National Geographic*] article concluded:

> . . . it will be a hard thing for the planet if . . . people are
> eating meat and driving gasoline-powered cars at the same

rate as Americans now do. It's too late to keep the new middle class of 2030 from being born; it's not too late to change how they and the rest of us will produce and consume food and energy.

"Secret agency memos made public by a lawsuit show that the overwhelming consensus even among the FDA's own scientists was that GMOs can create unpredictable, hard-to-detect side effects."

Genetically Modified Food Is Unsafe

Institute for Responsible Technology

The Institute for Responsible Technology (IRT) is a nonprofit organization whose mission is to educate policy makers and the public on the risks associated with genetically modified foods and crops. The institute offers several reasons to avoid genetically modified organisms (GMOs) in the following viewpoint. Several of the reasons cited are health related, including the assertion that in the nine years following the introduction of GMOs in 1996 food allergies, disorders such as autism, and chronic illnesses increased sharply. The IRT also notes environmental concerns, including damaging the habitat for monarch butterflies.

As you read, consider the following questions:

1. What are some of the health problems that the Institute for Responsible Technology claims stemmed from the introduction of GMOs in 1996?

2. How do GMOs harm the environment, according to the viewpoint?

3. What were some of the findings on crop yields in the study conducted by the International Assessment of Agricultural Knowledge, Science and Technology for Development?

The American Academy of Environmental Medicine (AAEM) urges doctors to prescribe non-GMO [genetically modified organism] diets for all patients. They cite animal studies showing organ damage, gastrointestinal and immune system disorders, accelerated aging, and infertility. Human studies show how genetically modified (GM) food can leave material behind inside us, possibly causing long-term problems. Genes inserted into GM soy, for example, can transfer into the DNA [deoxyribonucleic acid] of bacteria living inside us, and that the toxic insecticide produced by GM corn was found in the blood of pregnant women and their unborn fetuses.

Numerous health problems increased after GMOs were introduced in 1996. The percentage of Americans with three or more chronic illnesses jumped from 7% to 13% in just 9 years; food allergies skyrocketed, and disorders such as autism, reproductive disorders, digestive problems, and others are on the rise. Although there is not sufficient research to confirm that GMOs are a contributing factor, doctors' groups such as the AAEM tell us not to wait before we start protecting ourselves, and especially our children who are most at risk.

The American Public Health Association and American Nurses Association are among many medical groups that condemn the use of GM bovine growth hormone, because the milk from treated cows has more of the hormone IGF-1 (insulin-like growth factor 1)—which is linked to cancer.

GMOs contaminate—forever. GMOs cross-pollinate and their seeds can travel. It is impossible to fully clean up our contaminated gene pool. Self-propagating GMO pollution will outlast the effects of global warming and nuclear waste. The potential impact is huge, threatening the health of future generations. GMO contamination has also caused economic losses for organic and non-GMO farmers who often struggle to keep their crops pure.

GMOs increase herbicide use. Most GM crops are engineered to be "herbicide tolerant." . . . Monsanto, for example, sells Roundup Ready crops, designed to survive applications of their Roundup herbicide.

Between 1996 and 2008, US farmers sprayed an extra 383 million pounds of herbicide on GMOs. Overuse of Roundup results in "superweeds," resistant to the herbicide. This is causing farmers to use even more toxic herbicides every year. Not only does this create environmental harm, GM foods contain higher residues of toxic herbicides. Roundup, for example, is linked with sterility, hormone disruption, birth defects, and cancer.

Genetic engineering creates dangerous side effects. By mixing genes from totally unrelated species, genetic engineering unleashes a host of unpredictable side effects. Moreover, irrespective of the type of genes that are inserted, the very process of creating a GM plant can result in massive collateral damage that produces new toxins, allergens, carcinogens, and nutritional deficiencies.

Government oversight is dangerously lax. Most of the health and environmental risks of GMOs are ignored by governments' superficial regulations and safety assessments. The reason for this tragedy is largely political. The US Food and Drug Administration (FDA), for example, doesn't require a single safety study, does not mandate labeling of GMOs, and allows companies to put their GM foods on the market without even notifying the agency. Their justification was the claim that they had no information showing that GM foods were substantially different. But this was a lie. Secret agency memos made public by a lawsuit show that the overwhelming consensus even among the FDA's own scientists was that GMOs can create unpredictable, hard-to-detect side effects. They urged long-term safety studies. But the White House had instructed the FDA to promote biotechnology, and the agency official in charge of policy was Michael Taylor, Monsanto's former attorney, later their vice president. He's now the US food safety czar [the deputy commissioner for foods at the FDA].

The biotech industry uses "tobacco science" to claim product safety. Biotech companies like Monsanto told us that Agent Orange, PCBs [polychlorinated biphenyl], and DDT [dichlorodiphenyltrichloroethane] were safe. They are now using the same type of superficial, rigged research to try and convince us that GMOs are safe. Independent scientists, however, have caught the spin masters red-handed, demonstrating without doubt how industry-funded research is designed to avoid finding problems, and how adverse findings are distorted or denied.

Independent research and reporting is attacked and suppressed. Scientists who discover problems with GMOs have been attacked, gagged, fired, threatened, and denied funding. The journal *Nature* acknowledged that a "large block of scientists . . . denigrate research by other legitimate scientists in a knee-jerk, partisan, emotional way that is not helpful in advancing knowledge." Attempts by media to expose problems are also often censored.

GMOs harm the environment. GM crops and their associated herbicides can harm birds, insects, amphibians, marine ecosystems, and soil organisms. They reduce biodiversity, pollute water resources, and are unsustainable. For example, GM crops are eliminating habitat for monarch butterflies, whose populations are down 50% in the US. Roundup herbicide has been shown to cause birth defects in amphibians, embryonic deaths and endocrine disruptions, and organ damage in animals even at very low doses. GM canola has been found growing wild in North Dakota and California, threatening to pass on its herbicide-tolerant genes on to weeds.

GMOs do not increase yields and work against feeding a hungry world. Whereas sustainable non-GMO agricultural methods used in developing countries have conclusively resulted in yield increases of 79% and higher, GMOs do not, on average, increase yields at all. This was evident in the Union of Concerned Scientists' 2009 report "Failure to Yield"—the definitive study to date on GM crops and yield.

The International Assessment of Agricultural Knowledge, Science and Technology for Development (IAASTD) report, authored by more than 400 scientists and backed by 58 governments, stated that GM crop yields were "highly variable" and in some cases, "yields declined." The report noted, "Assessment of the technology lags behind its development, information is anecdotal and contradictory, and uncertainty about possible benefits and damage is unavoidable." They determined that the current GMOs have nothing to offer the goals of reducing hunger and poverty; improving nutrition, health and rural livelihoods; and facilitating social and environmental sustainability.

On the contrary, GMOs divert money and resources that would otherwise be spent on more safe, reliable, and appropriate technologies.

By avoiding GMOs, you contribute to the coming tipping point of consumer rejection, forcing them out of our food supply. Because GMOs give no consumer benefits, if even a small percentage of us start rejecting brands that contain them, GM ingredients will become a marketing liability. Food companies will kick them out. In Europe, for example, the tipping point was achieved in 1999, just after a high-profile GMO safety scandal hit the papers and alerted citizens to the potential dangers. In the US, a consumer rebellion against GM bovine growth hormone has also reached a tipping point, and kicked the cow drug out of dairy products by Walmart, Starbucks, Dannon, Yoplait, and most of America's dairies.

The Campaign for Healthier Eating in America is designed to achieve a tipping point against GMOs in the US. The number of non-GMO shoppers needed is probably just 5% of the population. The key is to educate consumers about the documented health dangers and provide a non-GMO shopping guide to make avoiding GMOs much easier.

*"The scientific consensus is that health
and safety are simply not an issue."*

Genetically Modified Food
Is Healthy

Shanley Chien

*Shanley Chien is a student at Northwestern University's Medill
School of Journalism. In the following viewpoint, Chien argues
that despite the agreement among most scientists that genetically
modified organisms (GMOs) are just as safe as food grown by
conventional methods, advocacy groups have convinced many
members of the public that GMOs are unhealthy. Chien cites research conducted on more than one hundred billion animals that
were given genetically engineered and non–genetically engineered
animal feed that concludes both are equally safe. Although there
is some evidence that the overuse of some biological pesticides
has resulted in insect and weed resistance, this has occurred for
many years with conventional pesticides as well, Chien contends.*

As you read, consider the following questions:

1. What are some of the reasons why it is not scientifically defensible to call a crop GMO free, according to the viewpoint?

2. According to the viewpoint, what are the three common types of genetic engineering?

3. What are some of the reasons why weeds and insects develop a resistance to chemicals, according to the viewpoint?

You walk down the aisles at Whole Foods spotting milk, cookies, pasta, and a variety of other products with the "Non-GMO Project Verified" label. The label tells you the foods don't contain genetically modified organisms—GMOs.

Anti-GMO Crusaders Mislead the Public

But the image of a butterfly sitting on a blade of grass shaped like a check mark subconsciously reassures you that this product is "safe." After all, if it's safe enough for a butterfly, it's safe enough for you and your family. You put it in your basket, perhaps because people like Dr. [Mehmet] Oz and food blogger Vani Hari of *Food Babe* tell you GMOs are unhealthy.

GMOs add to the nutritional value and preservation of foods and most scientists vouch for their safety. But critics abound.

"We have the whole government working against us," Hari said in an interview on Carolina Connection talk radio. "They don't want Americans to figure out that these could be causing health issues, that they haven't been tested, and they are increasing pesticide and herbicide use."

Organizations and advocacy groups such as the Non-GMO Project, Dr. Oz, *Food Babe*, and other anti-GMO crusaders say GMOs are unnatural and unhealthy, according to their websites.

Recently, Hershey's announced it will remove all genetically engineered (GE) ingredients from its popular lineup of candy bars by the end of the year [2015]. Social media, emails, and phone calls from consumers and the anti-GMO advocacy group GMO Inside pressured the company into making the move away from GE ingredients, GMO Inside stated in a press release.

The group also reported that Hershey's will replace GM sugar beet with cane sugar and use a non-GM version of soy lecithin. Hershey's new initiative to "make [its] products using ingredients that are simple and easy-to-understand" also means there won't be any more artificial flavors or high fructose corn syrup, and will be gluten free, the group said.

"I think if you don't know much about [the science], it's very easy to be misled by groups who appear to have an interest in protecting you," said Dr. Alison Van Eenennaam, professor of animal biotechnology and genomics at the University of California, Davis.

A "GMO Free" Claim Is Hard to Prove

According to the Non-GMO Project's website, the company earns more than $11 billion in annual sales and has more than 27,000 products verified with its seal. But purchasing a product with the "Non-GMO Project Verified" stamp doesn't necessarily mean your food is GMO free: The company states its verification seal "is not a 'GMO free' claim."

"Given the high number of specific, key commodity GMO crops (soy, corn, sugar beet, canola, cotton, alfalfa, etc.), it's not scientifically or legally defensible to call something GMO free," said Caroline Kinsman, communications manager at the Non-GMO Project.

Kinsman explained that the Non-GMO Project provides a "rigorous voluntary verification program for GMO avoidance," using a polymerase chain reaction (PCR) test to determine whether or not a raw ingredient contains GMO content.

PCR testing replicates a piece of DNA [deoxyribonucleic acid] and makes thousands to millions of copies of that specific segment so machines can detect any traces, but this method can only be used if tested at the raw-ingredient level.

"Say I'm making a chocolate chip cookie. A test is basically going to look for DNA in the final cookie product," Van Eenennaam said. "In this cookie there would be sugar, and sugar can be derived from GE sugar beets or it might be derived from non-GE sugar cane, but there's no way they'd be able to [scientifically] test that [in the final stage]."

Amid the heated public debate and confusion, it's important to understand what exactly GMOs are.

Common Types of Genetic Engineering

Dennis Halterman, research geneticist at the U.S. Department of Agriculture's [USDA's] Agricultural Research Service and University of Wisconsin-Madison, has dedicated his career to how plants interact with pathogens on a molecular level and used GMO technology to develop a natural plant resistance to diseases without the use of chemicals.

He explained that humans have been genetically modifying food since the beginning of agriculture and there are now various methods to safely genetically engineer thanks to new science.

The most traditional way is crossbreeding, which entails taking the flowers and pollen from a plant that has a desired trait (like resistance to viruses, fungi, bacteria, etc.) and crossing them with another plant that is susceptible but has other good traits (like high yield). This process for creating hybrids has been used since the dawn of agriculture and is done by planting various seeds in the field and seeing which ones grow with the desired traits.

With advanced biotechnology, scientists can now take specific genes and move them individually into a new variety by using agrobacterium, a type of natural soil bacteria that introduces a segment of its own DNA into the genome of a plant, carrying with it a specific set of instructions for the plant to carry out. Halterman explained that, although using agrobacterium still produces random results, scientists are able to counter the random nature of this method by playing the numbers game.

"We will make hundreds or thousands of plants, each with a different insertion of the gene and find the one out of all those that behaves as we expect it to," he said.

The USDA-approved non-browning Arctic apples that made the news last month [in February 2015] were achieved by another method of genetic modification called gene silencing. Over the past 10 to 15 years, scientists have used this method to "turn off" certain genes without introducing DNA that encodes a protein.

Instead, the process occurs at the ribonucleic acid level—RNA for short. RNA is a single-stranded molecule responsible for coding and expressing genes. Because many viruses produce double-stranded RNA (dsRNA) throughout their life cycle, plants can recognize the presence of dsRNA and, as a defense mechanism, eliminate it. Scientists discovered that they can use the plant's inherent defense system to control gene expression, by producing a dsRNA of a targeted gene that the plant will perceive as a virus and sending a signal to the plant's control center to chop up the sequence so that it can no longer function.

Additionally, new gene-editing technology is so advanced now that scientists can target exactly where they want to introduce a piece of DNA into the plant's genome. This precision allows them to more accurately insert, replace, or remove DNA in parts of a genome.

Benefits of GMOs

In the case of the Arctic apples, turning off the gene that controls browning would help limit food waste for consumers and the planet. Approximately 40 percent of food produced in the U.S. goes to waste as it passes through the food supply chain, according to a study conducted by the U.S. Environmental Protection Agency. This scientific advancement has the potential to mitigate that issue.

But the technological advancements scientists have made in recent years in GMOs not only benefit farmers; they also help to alleviate the increasing global population and third world hunger, Halterman said.

According to the United Nations World Food Programme, "some 805 million people in the world do not have enough food to lead a healthy, active life. That's about one in nine people on earth." Additionally, "poor nutrition causes nearly half (45 percent) of deaths in children under five—3.1 million children each year."

Scientists were not only able to create a genetically engineered fortified grain to combat vitamin A deficiency (called golden rice), but they can also help hunger-stricken nations that don't have access to the same pesticides as the U.S. and other first world nations still be able to grow high-yield crops that resist drought, insects, and diseases, Halterman said.

Risks of GMOs

Of course, GMOs are not without problems, as well. Like many big issues, the topic of GMOs is very nuanced, especially when you throw in corporate farming giants like Monsanto—a leading agricultural biotech company of GE seeds and herbicide brand Roundup—dominating the market share.

"On the food safety side, I personally don't have any concerns based on the published literature with the safety of the products that are out on the market right now," said Dr. Peggy Lemaux, professor of crop biotechnology at the University of California, Berkeley. "But I do have some issues with the speed with which things have come out and also the repetitive nature of the changes they've made."

Lemaux referred to the overuse of certain technology, like Monsanto's Roundup Ready and the biological pesticide *Bacillus thuringiensis* (or Bt), for herbicide tolerance and insect resistance in crops.

"Because a lot of these have been used over and over again, year after year, in the same crops and in the same field, insects and weeds develop resistance. They mutate," she said.

Although Monsanto states on its website that "GM crops have been reviewed and tested [...] and have been shown to be as safe as conventional crops," it acknowledges that there are potential challenges based around resistance that need to be addressed. The company stated in a press release that there are a small number of insects that have a preexisting resistance to certain Bt proteins. But with current farming practices, "it is possible that too many insects in a field could develop a tolerance to a Bt protein and cause significant damage or destruction."

Although a valid concern, other scientists—including Halterman and Van Eenennaam—have attributed that insect and weed resistance to the basic concepts of agriculture and evolution.

Weed and insect resistance is "absolutely a concern, but people have been aware of that forever anyway," Halterman said. "It doesn't matter what the pesticide or herbicide is. That's not anything new. We'd be concerned if we weren't using Roundup and were using something more dangerous like 2,4-d [dichlorophenoxyacetic acid] or more toxic chemicals. We'd still be stuck with weed resistance."

"Weeds developed a resistance to those chemicals because weeds evolve over time—as do insects, as does everything," Van Eenennaam said. "They evolve around different control mechanisms, even mechanical mechanisms."

She used the example of using a mower to take care of weeds and how they've developed so that, instead of sprouting

Common Types of Genetic Engineering

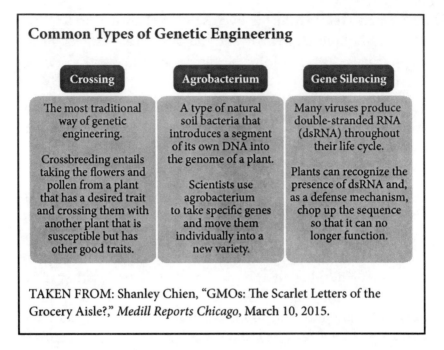

Crossing	Agrobacterium	Gene Silencing
The most traditional way of genetic engineering. Crossbreeding entails taking the flowers and pollen from a plant that has a desired trait and crossing them with another plant that is susceptible but has other good traits.	A type of natural soil bacteria that introduces a segment of its own DNA into the genome of a plant. Scientists use agrobacterium to take specific genes and move them individually into a new variety.	Many viruses produce double-stranded RNA (dsRNA) throughout their life cycle. Plants can recognize the presence of dsRNA and, as a defense mechanism, chop up the sequence so that it can no longer function.

TAKEN FROM: Shanley Chien, "GMOs: The Scarlet Letters of the Grocery Aisle?," *Medill Reports Chicago*, March 10, 2015.

up to a stalk, they spread across the ground so they avoid getting cut by the blade and the mower.

"Weeds are always developing resistance to things, so this idea that GMOs are uniquely associated with the development of resistance is [odd]," she said, adding that herbicide resistance can be alleviated by rotating chemical herbicide usage with other weed control techniques.

Physiology and GMOs

"We think there is no argument on health and safety," said Karen Batra, director of communications at Biotechnology Industry Organization, who speaks on behalf of the biotech industry (including Monsanto). "The scientific consensus is that health and safety are simply not an issue. Any food product containing genetically modified ingredients are exactly as healthy and safe as their conventional counterparts."

Monsanto also stated in a press release that they conduct extensive tests to determine the safety of their products. Kevin

Glenn, product safety center lead at Monsanto, said they supplement their evaluation by studying the toxicology and physiology of the rats to determine if there could be any adverse effects on humans.

"All of these assessments have some known association with important health or physiological function in the animal that would be impacted and give us a clue if there is some toxicity," Glenn said.

Glenn and other third-party scientists said there are currently no commercialized biotech products that have been associated with "an actual hazard to humans or animals." Yet, even with all the evidence showing GMOs don't pose health risks, the scientific community still struggles to convince the public of GMOs' safety.

The divisive tension between the anti-GMO and pro-GMO camps leaves many people uncertain about their food choices, especially about the health effects of consuming GM food, and wondering if they pass along a piece of DNA they ingested to their children. But Lemaux said there's a flaw in that way of thinking.

"We've been eating genes since the beginning of time. Everything we eat, particular fresh stuff, has [foreign] genes and DNA," Lemaux said. "This process happens all the time: We're eating genes and DNA, and they all get broken down. So the genes are not going to go through your small intestine wall and somehow go through your veins and get into your blood. It's just not going to happen."

Van Eenennaam conducted an in-depth literature review of 29 years' worth of animal productivity and health information. After studying field data of over 100 billion animals given non-GE and GE animal feed, she discovered that there are no health risks. She said scientists have published long-term studies of animals on GE-based diets and concluded "that GM plants are nutritionally equivalent to their non-GM counterparts and can be safely used in food and feed."

Oklahoma State University's Department of Agricultural Economics published a survey in January 2015 that showed 82 percent of people wanted food with GMOs to be labeled, an initiative that the California state senate voted down last year.

But the survey also showed that just as many people (80 percent) also supported mandatory labeling for foods containing deoxyribonucleic acid, more commonly known as DNA. Considering that all food has DNA, these results are indicative of the general population's lack of scientific knowledge.

"If you're starting at that level of information with people, then having them understand scientific studies that were done [. . .] is very difficult," Lemaux said.

But if beloved science educator Bill Nye the Science Guy can change his mind about GMOs, maybe GMOs are turning the tide.

"There's a chapter in [my book] which I'm going to revise," said Nye backstage after his appearance on HBO's *Real Time with Bill Maher* on Feb. 20. "It's about genetically modified food," he said. "And I'm very excited about telling the world. When you're in love you want to tell the world."

"The truth is, we don't know enough about GMOs to deem them safe for human consumption."

Genetically Modified Food Is Unhealthy

Arjun Walia

Arjun Walia is a writer for the alternative media website Collective-Evolution.com. In the following viewpoint, Walia reports on ten studies alleging that genetically modified organisms (GMOs) can be harmful to human health. The studies he cites link GMOs to illnesses and disorders such as gluten intolerance, breast cancer, birth defects, autism, Parkinson's disease, and Alzheimer's disease. GMOs have been around for only twenty years, he concludes, and this is not enough time to determine if they are safe.

As you read, consider the following questions:

1. What five conditions can be either triggered or exacerbated by GM foods, according to a study released by the Institute for Responsible Technology?

2. What is a xenoestrogen, and what are some of the problems it can cause, according to the viewpoint?

3. What happens when glyphosate is ingested, according to Walia?

Over the past few years, a number of countries have completely banned GMOs and the pesticides that go along with them, and they are doing so for a reason. The latest country to consider a complete ban is Russia after top government scientists recommended at least a 10-year ban.

The truth is, we don't know enough about GMOs to deem them safe for human consumption. Believe it or not, the very first commercial sale of them was only twenty years ago. There is no possible way that our health authorities can test all possible combinations on a large enough population, over a long enough period of time, to be able to say with absolute certainty that they are harmless.

There are a multitude of credible scientific studies that clearly demonstrate why GMOs should not be consumed and more are emerging every year. There are also a number of scientists all around the world that oppose them.

By slipping it into our food without our knowledge, without any indication that there are genetically modified organisms in our food, we are now unwittingly part of a massive experiment. The FDA [US Food and Drug Administration] has said that genetically modified organisms are not much different from regular food, so they'll be treated in the same way. The problem is this, geneticists follow the inheritance of genes, what biotechnology allows us to do is to take this organism, and move it horizontally into a totally unrelated species. Now David Suzuki doesn't normally mate with a carrot and exchange genes, what biotechnology allows us to do is to switch genes from one to the other without regard to the biological constraints. It's very very bad science; we assume that the principles governing the inheritance of genes vertically, applies when you move genes laterally or horizontally. There's absolutely no reason to make that conclusion—Geneticist David Suzuki

If anybody ever tells you that we know with one hundred percent certainty that GMOs are totally safe to eat, they haven't done their research. There is no reason GM foods should be approved safe for consumption; we just don't know enough about them. We could easily feed the planet through organic, GMO-free methods; there is absolutely no reason we need GM foods around. . . .

Multiple Toxins from GMOs Detected in Maternal and Fetal Blood

Research from Canada (the first of its kind) has successfully identified the presence of pesticides associated with genetically modified foods in maternal, fetal and non-pregnant women's blood. They also found the presence of Monsanto's Bt [*Bacillus thuringiensis*] toxin. The study was published in the journal *Reproductive Toxicology* in 2011.

> "Given the potential toxicity of these environmental pollutants and the fragility of the fetus, more studies are needed, particularly those using the placental transfer approach. Thus, our present results will provide baseline data for future studies exploring a new area of research relating to nutrition, toxicology and reproduction in women. Today, obstetric-gynecological disorders that are associated with environmental chemicals are not known. Thus, knowing the actual concentration of genetically modified foods in humans constitutes a cornerstone in the advancement of research in this area."

The study used blood samples from thirty pregnant women and thirty non-pregnant women. The study also pointed out that the fetus is considered to be highly susceptible to the adverse effects of xenobiotics (foreign chemical substance found within an organism that is not naturally produced). This is why the study emphasizes that knowing more about GMOs is crucial, because environmental agents could disrupt the biological events that are required to ensure normal growth and development.

DNA from Genetically Modified Crops Can Be Transferred into Humans Who Eat Them

In a new study published in the peer-reviewed *Public Library of Science (PLOS [One])* researchers emphasize that there is sufficient evidence that meal-derived DNA [deoxyribonucleic acid] fragments carry complete genes that can enter into the human circulation system through an *unknown* mechanism.

In one of the blood samples, the relative concentration of plant DNA was higher than the human DNA. The study was based on the analysis of over 1000 human samples from four independent studies. *PLOS [One]* is an open-access, well-respected peer-reviewed scientific journal that covers primary research from disciplines within science and medicine. It's great to see this study published in it, confirming what many have been suspecting for years.

"Our bloodstream is considered to be an environment well separated from the outside world and the digestive tract. According to the standard paradigm, large macromolecules consumed with food cannot pass directly to the circulatory system. During digestion, proteins and DNA are thought to be degraded into small constituents, amino acids and nucleic acids, respectively, and then absorbed by a complex active process and distributed to various parts of the body through the circulation system. Here, based on the analysis of over 1000 human samples from four independent studies, we report evidence that meal-derived DNA fragments which are large enough to carry complete genes can avoid degradation and through an unknown mechanism enter the human circulation system. In one of the blood samples, the relative concentration of plant DNA is higher than the human DNA. The plant DNA concentration shows a surprisingly precise log-normal distribution in the plasma samples while non-plasma (cord blood) control sample was found to be free of plant DNA."

This still doesn't mean that GMOs can enter into our cells, but given the fact that GMOs have been linked to cancer . . . it is safe to assume it is indeed a possibility. The bottom line is that we don't know, and this study demonstrates another cause for concern.

New Study Links GMOs to Gluten Disorders That Affect Millions of Americans

This study was recently released by the Institute for Responsible Technology (IRT) and uses data from the US Department of Agriculture, US Environmental Protection Agency, [and] medical journal reviews as well as other independent research. The authors relate GM foods to five conditions that may either trigger or exacerbate gluten-related disorders, including the autoimmune disorder, celiac disease:

- Intestinal permeability

- Imbalanced gut bacteria

- Immune activation and allergic response

- Impaired digestion

- Damage to the intestinal wall

The Institute for Responsible Technology is a world leader in educating policy makers and the public about GMO foods and crops. The institute reports and investigates on the impact GM foods can have on health, environment, agriculture and more.

Study Links Genetically Modified Corn to Rat Tumors

In November 2012, the journal *Food and Chemical Toxicology* published a paper titled "Long-term toxicity of a Roundup herbicide and a Roundup-tolerant genetically modified maize" by Gilles-Éric Séralini and his team of researchers at France's Caen University.

It was a very significant study, which obviously looks bad for the big biotech companies like Monsanto, being the first and only long-term study under controlled conditions examining the possible effects of a diet of GMO maize treated with Monsanto Roundup herbicide.

This study has since been retracted, which is odd, because the journal it was published in is a very well-known, reputable peer-reviewed scientific journal. In order for a study to be published here it has to go through a rigorous review process.

It's also important to note that hundreds of scientists from around the world have condemned the retraction of the study. This study was done by experts, and a correlation between GMOs and these tumors can't be denied. . . .

The multiple criticisms of the study have also been answered by the team of researchers that conducted the study. . . .

Glyphosate Linked to Birth Defects

A group of scientists put together a comprehensive review of existing data that shows how European regulators have known that Monsanto's glyphosate causes a number of birth malformations since at least 2002. Regulators misled the public about glyphosate's safety, and in Germany the Federal Office of Consumer Protection and Food Safety told the European Commission that there was no evidence to suggest that glyphosate causes birth defects.

> Our examination of the evidence leads us to the conclusion that the current approval of glyphosate and Roundup is

Getting Ill from GMO Corn

When I first came to allergist Paris Mansmann, ... I was 36. I'd been sick for three and a half years. ...

I had no diagnosis, just a collection of weird symptoms: tight, achy pain that radiated through my body and caused me to hobble around; burning rashes that splashed across my cheeks and around my mouth like pizza sauce; exhaustion; headaches; hands that froze into claws while I slept and hurt to uncurl in the morning; a constant head cold; nausea; and, on top of all that, severe insomnia—my body just could not, would not, turn off and rest. I visited every doctor who'd see me and tried everything they threw at me. ...

After escorting me into an exam room, he sat down across from me and promptly pushed aside my thick medical file. He'd read through it all, he said, but he wanted to hear the story from me. He listened patiently. ... Then, with no pyrotechnics, he offered his theory: "I think it's possible you've developed a reaction to genetically modified corn."

Caitlin Shetterly, "The Bad Seed:
The Health Risks of Genetically Modified Corn,"
Elle, July 24, 2013.

deeply flawed and unreliable. In this report, we examine the industry studies and regulatory documents that led to the approval of glyphosate. We show that industry and regulators knew as long ago as the 1980s and 1990s that glyphosate causes malformation—but that this information was not made public. We demonstrate how EU regulators reasoned their way from clear evidence of glyphosate's teratogenicity in the industry's own studies to a conclusion that minimized these findings in the EU Commission's final review report.

Here is a summary of the report:

- Multiple peer-reviewed scientific literature documenting serious health hazards posed by glyphosate

- Industry (including Monsanto) has known since the 1980s that glyphosate causes malformations in experimental animals at high doses

- Industry has known since 1993 that these effects could also occur at lower and mid doses

- The German government has known since at least 1998 that glyphosate causes malformations

- The [European] Commission's expert scientific review panel knew in 1999 that glyphosate causes malformations

- The [European] Commission has known since 2002 that glyphosate causes malformations. . . .

Another study published by the American Chemical Society, from the University of Buenos Aires, Argentina, also showed that glyphosate can cause abnormalities.

The direct effect of glyphosate on early mechanisms of morphogenesis in vertebrate embryos opens concerns about the clinical findings from human offspring in populations exposed to glyphosate in agricultural fields.

Study Links Glyphosate to Autism, Parkinson's Disease, and Alzheimer's Disease

When you ingest glyphosate, you are in essence altering the chemistry of your body. It's completely unnatural and the body doesn't resonate with it. [Cytochrome] P450 (CYP) is the gene pathway disrupted when the body takes in glyphosate. [Cytochrome] P450 creates enzymes that assist with the formation of molecules in cells, as well as breaking them down. CYP enzymes are abundant and have many important functions. They are responsible for detoxifying xenobiotics from the body, things like the various chemicals found in pesticides, drugs and carcinogens. Glyphosate inhibits the CYP enzymes. The CYP pathway is critical for normal, natural functioning of multiple biological systems within our bodies. Because humans that've been exposed to glyphosate have a drop in amino acid tryptophan levels, they do not have the necessary active signaling of the neurotransmitter serotonin, which is associated with weight gain, depression and Alzheimer's disease.

Chronically Ill Humans Have Higher Glyphosate Levels than Healthy Humans

A new study out of Germany concludes that glyphosate residue could reach humans and animals through feed and can be excreted in urine. It outlines how presence of glyphosate in urine and its accumulation in animal tissues is alarming even at low concentrations.

> To this day, Monsanto continues to advertise its Roundup products as environmentally friendly and claims that neither animals nor humans are affected by this toxin. Environmentalists, veterinarians, medical doctors and scientists, however, have raised increasing alarms about the danger of glyphosate in the animal and human food chain as well as the environment. The fact that glyphosate has been found in animals and humans is of great concern. In the search for the causes of serious diseases amongst entire herds of animals in northern Germany, especially cattle, glyphosate has repeatedly been detected in the urine, feces, milk and feed of the animals. Even more alarming glyphosate was detected in the urine of the farmers.

Studies Link GMO Animal Feed to Severe Stomach Inflammation and Enlarged Uteri in Pigs

A study by scientist Judy Carman, PhD, that was recently published in the peer-reviewed *Journal of Organic Systems* outlines the effects of a diet mixed with GMO feed for pigs, and how it is a cause for concern when it comes to health. Scientists randomized and fed isowean [short for isolated weaning] pigs either a mixed GM soy and GM corn (maize) diet for approximately 23 weeks (nothing out of the ordinary for most pigs in the United States), which is unfortunately the normal life span of a commercial pig from weaning to slaughter. Equal numbers of male and female pigs were present in each group. The GM diet was associated with gastric and uterine differences in pigs. GM pigs had uteri that were 25% heavier than non-GM fed pigs. GM-fed pigs had a higher rate of severe stomach inflammation with a rate of 32% compared to 125 of non-GM fed pigs.

The study concluded that pigs fed a GMO diet exhibited a heavier uteri and a higher rate of severe stomach inflammation than pigs who weren't fed a GMO diet. Because the use of GMO feed for livestock and humans is so widespread, this is definitely another cause for concern when it comes to GMO consumption. Humans have a similar gastrointestinal tract to pigs, and these GM crops are consumed widely by people, especially in the United States.

GMO Risk Assessment Is Based on Very Little Scientific Evidence

Deficiencies have been revealed numerous times with regard to testing GM foods. [According to researchers Javier A. Magaña-Gómez and Ana M. Calderón de la Barca,]

> The first guidelines were originally designed to regulate the introduction of GM microbes and plants into the environ-

ment with no attention being paid to food safety concerns. However, they have been widely cited as adding authoritative scientific support to food safety assessment. Additionally, the statement of policy released by the Food and Drug Administration of the United States, presumptively recognizing the GM foods as GRAS (generally recognized as safe), was prepared while there were critical guidelines prepared by the International Life Sciences Institute Europe and FAO [Food and Agriculture Organization of the United Nations]/ WHO [World Health Organization] recommend that safety evaluation should be based on the concept of substantial equivalence, considering parameters such as molecular characterization, phenotypic characteristics, key nutrients, toxicants and allergens. Since 2003, official standards for food safety assessment have been published by the Codex Alimentarius commission of FAO/WHO. Published reviews with around 25 peer-reviewed studies have found that despite the guidelines, the risk assessment of GM foods has not followed a defined prototype.

The risk assessment of genetically modified (GM) crops for human nutrition and health has not been systematic. Evaluations for each GM crop or trait have been conducted using different feeding periods, animal models and parameters. The most common result is that GM and conventional sources include similar nutritional performance and growth in animals. However, adverse microscopic and molecular effects of some GM foods in different organs or tissues have been reported. While there are currently no standardized methods to evaluate the safety of GM foods, attempts toward harmonization are on the way. More scientific effort is necessary in order to build confidence in the evaluation and acceptance of GM foods.

So, if anybody ever tells you that GMOs are completely safe for consumption, it's not true. We just don't know enough about them to make such a definitive statement. A lot of evidence actually points to the contrary.

Periodical and Internet Sources Bibliography

The following articles have been selected to supplement the diverse views presented in this chapter.

Molly Ball — "Want to Know If Your Food Is Genetically Modified?," *Atlantic*, May 14, 2014.

Morgan Chilson — "GMO Foods: Are They Safe?," Newsmax Health, June 3, 2015.

Jon Entine — "The Debate About GMO Safety Is Over, Thanks to a New Trillion-Meal Study," *Forbes*, September 17, 2014.

Mark Hertsgaard — "How to Feed the World After Climate Change," *Slate*, November 16, 2015.

Nathanael Johnson — "Golden Rice: Fool's Gold or Golden Opportunity?," *Grist*, August 29, 2013.

Layla Katiraee — "10 Studies Proving GMOs Are Harmful? Not If Science Matters," Genetic Literacy Project, November 13, 2015.

Andrew Kimbrell — "The Case for Labeling GMOs," *U.S. News & World Report*, November 4, 2013.

Jonathan Knutson — "GMO Food Is Safe, Scientist Says," *Grand Forks Herald* (North Dakota), June 23, 2015.

Thomas Kostigen — "Genetic Modification Can Help Solve Food Crisis," MarketWatch, November 16, 2012.

Mark Lynas — "How I Got Converted to G.M.O. Food," *New York Times*, April 24, 2015.

Scientific American — "Labels for GMO Foods Are a Bad Idea," August 20, 2013.

Marta Tellado — "GMO Labels Make Good Sense," CNN, June 25, 2015.

Is Water Scarcity a Threat to Global Sustainability?

Chapter Preface

In 1976 bottled water was a niche industry in the United States, with consumers drinking about 1.6 gallons of bottled water per capita per year. By 2014 bottled water was a major global business, with the average American drinking 34 gallons of bottled water each year. A $5 million marketing campaign launched by the makers of Perrier bottled mineral water to increase sales in the US market is generally credited by industry analysts as the turning point. The campaign, which played on Americans' fear of pollution and poor water quality, grew Perrier's sales from 12 million bottles in 1980 to 152 million in 1990. By 2014 the bottled water industry was a $13 billion business in the United States, with Americans consuming 11 billion gallons of bottled water in more than 30 billion plastic water bottles. More than half of the population of the United States drinks bottled water, and it represents 30 percent of all liquid refreshment sales, second only to soft drinks.

Since approximately 50 percent of all bottled water is actually tap water, what accounts for its popularity? According to the website Food Manufacturing, "There are many reasons for consumer enthusiasm for bottled water, including its association with healthfulness, convenience, safety, and value."

Among the controversies surrounding global water supply is the popularity of bottled water and its safety and impact on the environment. According to the Pacific Institute, it takes three liters of water to package one liter of bottled water; producing the bottles for US consumption requires more than 17 million barrels of oil; and bottling water produces more than 2.5 million tons of carbon dioxide. Although water bottles are made of polyethylene terephthalate (PET) plastic, which is recyclable, only 20 percent of all water bottles in the United States are recycled. PET is not biodegradable; it breaks down into smaller fragments over time, with the fragments absorbing toxins that pollute the environment and harm animals.

Ironically, while bottled water producers have marketed it as a safer alternative to tap water, tap water is monitored under the strict standards of the Environmental Protection Agency (EPA), and bottled water is not. As a result of laxer standards, bottled water can be harmful. According to Norm Schriever writing for the *Huffington Post*, "Plastic leaches into the water it holds, which has been linked to health issues like reproductive problems and different types of cancer. Harmful hormone-disrupting phthalates leach into the bottled water we drink after as little as 10 weeks of storage, or much faster once the bottles have been left in the sun (like in the car)."

Writing in *Friends Journal*, Charles Fager rebutted many of the arguments against bottled water. To those who claim that bottling wastes water supplies in its production, Fager argues, "all the bottled water in the U.S. accounts for less than one hundredth of one percent of water consumption. If it all disappeared tomorrow, this would have *no* measurable effect on the very real water problems the U.S. faces (ditto the world)." Fager responds to complaints about the environmental impact of plastic water bottles by predicting, "compostable water bottles made from plant products, without petroleum, are already coming onto the market, and bottled water in these containers is on sale in some areas. I predict it will soon be widely available in retail markets, providing a much more environmentally friendly option." In addition, he argues that plastic water bottles are much safer than their primary alternative—glass containers—and bottled water is an essential lifesaver in natural disasters.

The impact of water bottles is just one of the concerns in the larger issue of worldwide water scarcity. In the following chapter, scientists, journalists, and researchers debate whether water scarcity is a threat to global sustainability.

> *"Unless the balance between demand and finite supplies is restored, the world will face an increasingly severe global water deficit."*

There Is a Global Water Crisis

United Nations World Water Assessment Programme

Hosted and led by the United Nations Educational, Scientific and Cultural Organization (UNESCO), the United Nations World Water Assessment Programme (WWAP) coordinates the work of twenty-eight WWAP members and partners in "The United Nations World Water Development Report." In the following viewpoint, WWAP argues that water is at the core of sustainable development. There are three dimensions to sustainable development—poverty and social equity, economic development, and environmental protection and ecosystem services—and each of these is dependent on an adequate worldwide water supply, WWAP contends. The worldwide water supply will be challenged by population growth, climate change, and development and economic growth. Steps must be taken to manage water resources to support human well-being and environmental sustainability, WWAP concludes.

As you read, consider the following questions:

1. According to WWAP, what are some of the factors influencing global water demand?

2. What are some of the key interlinkages between water and sustainable development, according to the viewpoint?

3. What are the five target areas of the Sustainable Development Goal regarding water, according to WWAP?

Water is at the core of sustainable development. Water resources, and the range of services they provide, underpin poverty reduction, economic growth and environmental sustainability. From food and energy security to human and environmental health, water contributes to improvements in social well-being and inclusive growth, affecting the livelihoods of billions.

In a sustainable world that is achievable in the near future, water and related resources are managed in support of human well-being and ecosystem integrity in a robust economy. Sufficient and safe water is made available to meet every person's basic needs, with healthy lifestyles and behaviours easily upheld through reliable and affordable water supply and sanitation services, in turn supported by equitably extended and efficiently managed infrastructure. Water resources management, infrastructure and service delivery are sustainably financed. Water is duly valued in all its forms, with wastewater treated as a resource that avails energy, nutrients and freshwater for reuse. Human settlements develop in harmony with the natural water cycle and the ecosystems that support it, with measures in place that reduce vulnerability and improve resilience to water-related disasters. Integrated approaches to water resources development, management and use—and to human rights—are the norm. Water is governed in a participatory way that draws on the full potential of women and men as professionals and citizens, guided by a number of able and knowledgeable organizations, within a just and transparent institutional framework.

The Consequences of Unsustainable Growth

Unsustainable development pathways and governance failures have affected the quality and availability of water resources, compromising their capacity to generate social and economic benefits. Demand for freshwater is growing. Unless the balance between demand and finite supplies is restored, the world will face an increasingly severe global water deficit.

Global water demand is largely influenced by population growth, urbanization, food and energy security policies, and macroeconomic processes such as trade globalization, changing diets and increasing consumption. By 2050, global water demand is projected to increase by 55%, mainly due to growing demands from manufacturing, thermal electricity generation and domestic use.

Competing demands impose difficult allocation decisions and limit the expansion of sectors critical to sustainable development, in particular food production and energy. The competition for water—between water "uses" and water "users"—increases the risk of localized conflicts and continued inequities in access to services, with significant impacts on local economies and human well-being.

Over-abstraction is often the result of outdated models of natural resource use and governance, where the use of resources for economic growth is under-regulated and undertaken without appropriate controls. Groundwater supplies are diminishing, with an estimated 20% of the world's aquifers currently overexploited. Disruption of ecosystems through unabated urbanization, inappropriate agricultural practices, deforestation and pollution are among the factors undermining the environment's capacity to provide ecosystem services, including clean water.

Persistent poverty, inequitable access to water supply and sanitation services, inadequate financing, and deficient information about the state of water resources, their use and management impose further constraints on water resources management and its ability to help achieve sustainable development objectives.

Water and the Three Dimensions of Sustainable Development

Progress in each of the three dimensions of sustainable development—social, economic and environmental—is bound by the limits imposed by finite and often vulnerable water resources and the way these resources are managed to provide services and benefits.

While access to household water supplies is critical for a family's health and social dignity, access to water for productive uses such as agriculture and family-run businesses is vital to realize livelihood opportunities, generate income and contribute to economic productivity. Investing in improved water management and services can help reduce poverty and sustain economic growth. Poverty-oriented water interventions can make a difference for billions of poor people who receive very direct benefits from improved water and sanitation services through better health, reduced health costs, increased productivity and time-savings.

Economic growth itself is not a guarantee for wider social progress. In most countries, there is a wide—and often widening—gap between rich and poor, and between those who can and cannot exploit new opportunities. Access to safe drinking water and sanitation is a human right, yet its limited realization throughout the world often has disproportionate impacts on the poor and on women and children in particular.

Water is an essential resource in the production of most types of goods and services including food, energy and manufacturing. Water supply (quantity and quality) at the place

89

where the user needs it must be reliable and predictable to support financially sustainable investments in economic activities. Wise investment in both hard and soft infrastructure that is adequately financed, operated and maintained facilitates the structural changes necessary to foster advances in many productive areas of the economy. This often means more income opportunities to enhance expenditure in health and education, reinforcing a self-sustained dynamic of economic development.

Many benefits may be gained by promoting and facilitating use of the best available technologies and management systems in water provision, productivity and efficiency, and by improving water allocation mechanisms. These types of interventions and investments reconcile the continuous increase in water use with the need to preserve the critical environmental assets on which the provision of water and the economy depends.

Most economic models do not value the essential services provided by freshwater ecosystems, often leading to unsustainable use of water resources and ecosystem degradation. Pollution from untreated residential and industrial wastewater and agricultural runoff also weakens the capacity of ecosystems to provide water-related services.

Ecosystems across the world, particularly wetlands, are in decline. Ecosystem services remain undervalued, under-recognized and underutilized within most current economic and resource management approaches. A more holistic focus on ecosystems for water and development that maintains a beneficial mix between built and natural infrastructure can ensure that benefits are maximized.

Economic arguments can make the preservation of ecosystems relevant to decision makers and planners. Ecosystem valuation demonstrates that benefits far exceed costs of water-related investments in ecosystem conservation. Valuation is also important in assessing trade-offs in ecosystem conservation and can be used to better inform development plans. Adoption of "ecosystem-based management" is key to ensuring water's long-term sustainability.

Water's Role in Addressing Critical Developmental Challenges

Interlinkages between water and sustainable development reach far beyond its social, economic and environmental dimensions. Human health, food and energy security, urbanization and industrial growth, as well as climate change are critical challenge areas where policies and actions at the core of sustainable development can be strengthened (or weakened) through water.

Lack of water supply, sanitation and hygiene (WASH) takes a huge toll on health and well-being and comes at a large financial cost, including a sizable loss of economic activity. In order to achieve universal access, there is a need for accelerated progress in disadvantaged groups and to ensure non-discrimination in WASH service provision. Investments in water and sanitation services result in substantial economic gains; in developing regions, the return on investment has been estimated at US$5 to US$28 per dollar. An estimated US$53 billion a year over a five-year period would be needed to achieve universal coverage—a small sum given this represented less than 0.1% of the 2010 global GDP [gross domestic product].

The increase in the number of people without access to water and sanitation in urban areas is directly related to the rapid growth of slum populations in the developing world and the inability (or unwillingness) of local and national governments to provide adequate water and sanitation facilities in these communities. The world's slum population, which is expected to reach nearly 900 million by 2020, is also more vulnerable to the impacts of extreme weather events. It is however possible to improve performance of urban water supply systems while continuing to expand the system and addressing the needs of the poor.

By 2050, agriculture will need to produce 60% more food globally, and 100% more in developing countries. As the current growth rates of global agricultural water demand are unsustainable, the sector will need to increase its water use efficiency by reducing water losses and, most importantly, increase crop productivity with respect to water. Agricultural water pollution, which may worsen with increased intensive agriculture, can be reduced through a combination of instruments, including more stringent regulation, enforcement and well-targeted subsidies.

Energy production is generally water intensive. Meeting ever growing demands for energy will generate increasing stress on freshwater resources with repercussions on other users, such as agriculture and industry. Since these sectors also require energy, there is room to create synergies as they develop together. Maximizing the water efficiency of power plant cooling systems and increasing the capacity of wind, solar PV [photovoltaic] and geothermal energy will be a key determinant in achieving a sustainable water future.

Global water demand for the manufacturing industry is expected to increase by 400% from 2000 to 2050, leading all other sectors, with the bulk of this increase occurring in emerging economies and developing countries. Many large corporations have made considerable progress in evaluating and reducing their water use and that of their supply chains. Small- and medium-sized enterprises are faced with similar water challenges on a smaller scale, but have fewer means and less ability to meet them.

The negative impacts of climate change on freshwater systems will most likely outweigh its benefits. Current projections show that crucial changes in the temporal and spatial distributing of water resources and the frequency and intensity of water-related disasters rise significantly with increasing greenhouse gas emissions. Exploitation of new data sources, better models and more powerful data analysis methods, as well as the design of adaptive management strategies, can help respond effectively to changing and uncertain conditions.

Regional Perspectives

The challenges at the interface of water and sustainable development vary from one region to another.

Increasing resource use efficiency, reducing waste and pollution, influencing consumption patterns and choosing appropriate technologies are the main challenges facing Europe and North America. Reconciling different water uses at the basin level and improving policy coherence nationally and across borders will be priorities for many years to come.

Sustainability in the Asia and the Pacific region is intimately linked with progress in access to safe water and sanitation; meeting water demands across multiple uses and mitigating the concurrent pollution loads; improving groundwater management; and increasing resilience to water-related disasters.

Water scarcity stands at the forefront when considering water-related challenges that impede progress toward sustainable development in the Arab region, where unsustainable consumption and over-abstraction of surface and groundwater resources contribute to water shortages and threaten long-term sustainable development. Options being adopted to enhance water supplies include water harvesting, wastewater reuse and solar energy desalination.

A major priority for the Latin America and the Caribbean region is to build the formal institutional capacity to manage water resources and bring sustainable integration of water resources management and use into socioeconomic development and poverty reduction. Another priority is to ensure the

Water Stress Is Widespread

By 2030, the Water Resources Group forecasts, global water requirements may outstrip sustainable use by 40 percent. And almost half the world's people will be living under severe water stress, predicts the Organisation for Economic Co-operation and Development.

Already, water stress—where the reliable water supply is being used up more quickly than it can be replenished—is widespread and is expected to increase significantly in the years ahead, particularly in North Africa, the Middle East. By 2050, according to the UN's Food and Agriculture Organization, 1 in 5 developing countries will face water shortages.

William Wheeler, "Global Water Crisis:
Too Little, Too Much, or Lack of a Plan?,"
Christian Science Monitor, *December 2, 2012.*

full realization of the human right to water and sanitation in the context of the post-2015 development agenda.

The fundamental aim for Africa is to achieve durable and vibrant participation in the global economy while developing its natural and human resources without repeating the negatives experienced on the development paths of some other regions. Currently only 5% of Africa's potential water resources are developed and average per capita storage is 200 m^3 (compared to 6,000 m^3 in North America). Only 5% of Africa's cultivated land is irrigated and less than 10% of hydropower potential is utilized for electricity generation.

Responses and Means of Implementation

The Millennium Development Goals (MDGs) were successful in rallying public, private and political support for global poverty reduction. With regard to water, the MDGs helped to foster greater efforts toward improving access to drinking water supply and sanitation. However, the experience of the MDGs shows that a thematically broader, more detailed and context-specific framework for water, beyond the issues of water supply and sanitation, is called for in the post-2015 development agenda.

In 2014, UN-Water recommended a dedicated Sustainable Development Goal for water comprised of five target areas: (i) WASH; (ii) water resources; (iii) water governance; (iv) water quality and wastewater management; and (v) water-related disasters. Such a focused water goal would create social, economic, financial and other benefits that greatly outweigh its costs. Benefits would extend to the development of health, education, agriculture and food production, energy, industry and other social and economic activities.

Achieving the Future We Want

The outcome document of the 2012 UN Conference on Sustainable Development (Rio+20), "The Future We Want," recognized that "water is at the core of sustainable development," but at the same time development and economic growth creates pressure on the resource and challenges water security for humans and nature. There also remain major uncertainties about the amount of water required to meet the demand for food, energy and other human uses, and to sustain ecosystems. These uncertainties are exacerbated by the impact of climate change.

Water management is the responsibility of many different decision makers in public and private sectors. The issue is how such shared responsibility can be turned into something constructive and elevated to a rallying point around which different stakeholders can gather and participate collectively to make informed decisions.

Progress in water-related governance calls for engaging a broad range of societal actors, through inclusive governance structures that recognize the dispersion of decision making across various levels and entities. It is, for example, imperative to acknowledge women's contributions to local water management and role in decision making related to water.

While many countries face stalled water reform, others have made great strides in implementing various aspects of integrated water resources management (IWRM), including decentralized management and the creation of river basin organizations. As IWRM implementation has too often been geared toward economic efficiency, there is a need to put more emphasis on issues of equity and environmental sustainability and adopt measures to strengthen social, administrative and political accountability.

Investing in all aspects of water resources management, services provision and infrastructure (development, operation and maintenance) can generate significant social and economic benefits. Spending on drinking water supply and sanitation is highly cost-effective on health grounds alone. Investments in disaster preparedness, improved water quality and wastewater management are also highly cost-effective. Distribution of costs and benefits among stakeholders is crucial for financial feasibility.

Water-related disasters, the most economically and socially destructive of all natural hazards, are likely to increase with climate change. Planning, preparedness and coordinated responses—including floodplain management, early warning systems and increased public awareness of risk—greatly improve the resilience of communities. Blending structural and nonstructural flood management approaches is particularly cost-effective.

Risks and various water-related security issues can also be reduced by technical and social approaches. There are a growing number of examples of reclaimed wastewater being used in agriculture, for irrigating municipal parks and fields, in industrial cooling systems, and in some cases safely mixed in with drinking water.

Existing assessments of water resources are often inadequate for addressing modern water demands. Assessments are necessary to make informed investment and management decisions, facilitate cross-sector decision making, and address compromises and trade-offs between stakeholder groups.

Social equity is one of the dimensions of sustainable development that has been insufficiently addressed in development and water policies. Sustainable development and human rights perspectives both call for reductions in inequities and tackling disparities in access to WASH services.

This calls for a reorientation of investment priorities and operational procedures to provide services and allocate water more equitably in society. A pro–poor pricing policy keeps costs as low as possible, while ensuring that water is paid for at a level that supports maintenance and potential expansion of the system.

Water pricing also provides signals for how to allocate scarce water resources to the highest-value uses—in financial terms or other types of benefits. Equitable pricing and water permits need to adequately assure that abstraction as well as releases of used water support efficient operations and environmental sustainability in ways that are adapted to the abilities and needs of industry and larger-scale irrigation as well as small-scale and subsistence farming activities.

The principle of equity, perhaps more than any technical recommendation, carries with it the promise of a more water-secure world for all.

VIEWPOINT

▌ *"All water problems are local."*

There Is Not a Global Water Crisis

Charles Fishman

Charles Fishman is a former metro and national reporter for the
Washington Post. *Since 1996, he has worked for* Fast Company
magazine. He is the author of The Big Thirst: The Secret Life
and Turbulent Future of Water *and* The Wal-Mart Effect: How
the World's Most Powerful Company Really Works—and How
It's Transforming the American Economy. *In the following
viewpoint, Fishman argues that there is no global water crisis
because water problems are local in nature, not worldwide.
Global problems include climate change and global economic crises, which impact people throughout the world no matter where
the problem arises, he explains. Communities have the power to
take action to solve their own water problems, Fishman contends. He says all that is lacking is awareness on the part of
communities that water is a problem within their ability to
solve.*

Charles Fishman, "Why There Is No 'Global Water Crisis' (and Why That Means Water
Problems Are More Urgent than Ever)," Poweringanation.org, July 10, 2012. Copyright
© 2012 by Powering a Nation. All rights reserved. Reproduced with permission.

As you read, consider the following questions:

1. According to Fishman, what are some truly global problems?

2. Why is it unhelpful to label water a global crisis, according to the viewpoint?

3. What is lacking in most communities' response to water problems, according to Fishman?

There is no global water crisis.

We hear more and more often about "the global water crisis." As someone who has spent the last five years traveling the US and the world trying to understand water problems, I think one of the most important things to understand is: There is no global water crisis.

Water Problems Are Local

Many places have serious, urgent, even deadly, water problems. In fact, thousands of places have water problems.

But the secret is this: All water problems are local.

The water problems of Texas and Atlanta, of Los Angeles and Barcelona, of China and northern Mexico—those problems are unrelated to each other.

They may be similar kinds of problems; there may be much Delhi can learn from Sydney. But water problems are happening right where they are happening—the causes are local, and the solutions are local, too.

That's the good news about water—and water problems.

If Atlanta takes its water scarcity problems seriously, and solves them, no one can undo that solution. And Atlanta doesn't have to wait for anyone else to solve its water problems—doesn't have to wait for permission, or attention.

That's what makes water issues so different from other truly "global" problems—the global economic crisis, the global climate crisis.

A New Approach to Water

Our water problems are real. Our approach to water must change, and we'll be happier if we realize that, and handle the change with creativity and forethought rather than confront it as a crisis. It's water we're talking about, so there will be no avoiding the change. What we can choose is the time and the approach and the level of panic. . . .

We desperately need a fresh way of thinking about water. Or, more realistically, a starting point for thinking about water. Most of us haven't ever thought about it very much. But we'll need a foundation for understanding water as water issues become more urgent. We'll need a framework for thinking about the fate of water, because the fate of water is our fate.

We are at the start of a new era of water, an era when we'll need to use water much more smartly. Most important, we should be at the start of an era of much greater water equality—an era when no one dies simply because they can't get water, of all deprivations. There's no excuse for public officials not making clean water for their citizens a top priority now. But the era of smart water should make drinking water easier and cheaper to provide even in challenging circumstances. . . .

For the parts of the world that have luxuriated in the golden age of water, the era of smart water need not be the start of an era in which water scarcity or water limits desiccate the way we live. Quite the contrary: Using the right water for the right purpose may well open our eyes to the kinds of untapped sources of water, starting with our own wastewater, that we routinely overlook now.

Charles Fishman, The Big Thirst: The Secret Life and Turbulent Future of Water. *New York: Free Press, 2011.*

The worldwide economic downturn was, truly, caused by bad decisions in New York and London, in Reykjavik and Washington and Athens. Everyone in North Carolina can pay their mortgage and rent on time; can pay their credit card bills on time—and residents of Raleigh and Wilmington can still be badly hurt by the economic downturn.

Similarly, California can pass rigorous, progressive air pollution rules—and yet the progress that California makes can be undone by a single month's construction of new coal plants in China.

Those truly are "global" problems—where the issues sweep away even people who behave impeccably.

Communities Have the Power to Solve Water Problems

Water doesn't work that way.

When a community—San Antonio, Texas, is a good example—decides to take its water fate into its own hands, that city or town discovers it has all the power it needs to solve this particular set of problems. Communities can assess their own real water needs; they can assess the state of their access to water, and do what they need to do to find new sources of water; most important, communities can decide they want to change the water culture of their town—how people think about water, how they use it, how they value it, what they pay for it.

Cities don't need permission to teach their residents to use water more smartly, to use less water, to use the right water for the right purpose. Cities don't need permission to institute programs of reuse.

And when a community fixes its water problems, when it plans for the future, poor water management by some other city that is a time zone, or an ocean, away can't undo the work that town has done.

I think labeling water issues "a global water crisis" is, in fact, a well-intentioned effort to activate us—to wake us up to the urgency of water issues. But, frankly, people already confront too many global crises. The global economic and climate crises, of course, the global immigration crisis, the global environmental crisis.

One more "global crisis" is one too many. In the case of water, I think rather than activating us, labeling it a "global crisis" does just the opposite: It discourages us. Oh, no, another global crisis. Something so big and inaccessible, we need really important people, in the really important cities, to tackle it.

But, in fact, water isn't on the agenda in many global capitals right now.

And most important, we can tackle our own water problems. That's one of the other things that is so clear when you travel the world talking to people about water. When people get frustrated with poor access to water, with leaky pipes or poor planning, they discover that *they themselves* have the power to solve their water problems.

Most communities have enough money to tackle their water problems, enough knowledge, even enough water.

All they lack—all *we* lack—is the forehead-slapping moment. An awareness that, for water at least, we can grab hold of the problem and solve it ourselves.

And, in fact, no one else is going to solve our water problems for us.

> "Climate change due to unabated green-house gas emissions within our century is likely to put 40 percent more people at risk of absolute water scarcity than would be without climate change."

Climate Change Contributes to Water Scarcity

Science Daily

Science Daily is a science news website. In the following view-point, the editors of Science Daily report that water scarcity is already a reality for many people in the world today, with 1 to 2 percent of the world's population living in a country where wa-ter is scarce. Future population growth coupled with climate change will put 40 percent more people at risk worldwide. Different regions of the world will be impacted differently, the editors suggest, with the Mediterranean, Middle East, southern United States, and southern China experiencing severe water shortages.

As you read, consider the following questions:

1. According to the viewpoint, how many people today live in countries with absolute water scarcity? What is this projected to grow to with the effects of population growth and climate change?

2. Why is water scarcity a threat to human development, according to the viewpoint?

3. What additional research is required on the link between climate change and water scarcity, according to the viewpoint?

Water scarcity impacts people's lives in many countries already today. Future population growth will increase the demand for freshwater even further. Yet in addition to this, on the supply side, water resources will be affected by projected changes in rainfall and evaporation. Climate change due to unabated greenhouse gas emissions within our century is likely to put 40 percent more people at risk of absolute water scarcity than would be without climate change, a new study shows by using an unprecedented number of impact models.

The analysis is to be published in a special issue of the *Proceedings of the National Academy of Sciences* that assembles first results of the Inter-Sectoral Impact Model Intercomparison Project (ISI-MIP), a unique community-driven effort to bring research on climate change impacts to a new level.

"The steepest increase of global water scarcity might happen between 2 and 3 degrees global warming above preindustrial levels, and this is something to be experienced within the next few decades unless emissions get cut soon," says lead author Jacob Schewe of the Potsdam Institute for Climate Impact Research. "It is well known that water scarcity increases, but our study is the first to quantify the relative share that climate change has in that, compared to—and adding to—the increase that is simply due to population growth."

From China to the United States: Huge Regional Differences of Future Water Availability

Today, between one and two people out of a hundred live in countries with absolute water scarcity. Population growth and climate change combined would increase this to about ten in a hundred at roughly 3 degrees global warming. Absolute water scarcity is defined as less than 500 cubic meters available per year and person—a level requiring extremely efficient water use techniques and management in order to be sufficient, which in many countries are not in place. For a comparison, the global average water consumption per person and year is roughly 1200 cubic meters, and significantly more in many industrialized countries.

As climate change is not uniform across the world, the regional differences of its impacts on water availability are huge. For example, the Mediterranean, Middle East, the southern USA, and southern China will very probably see a pronounced decrease of available water, according to the study. Southern India, western China and parts of eastern Africa might see substantial increases.

Food Security Depends on Irrigation— Farmers Are Main Water Users

"Water scarcity is a major threat for human development, as for instance, food security in many regions depends on irrigation—agriculture is the main water user worldwide," says co-author Qiuhong Tang of the Chinese Academy of Sciences. "Still, an increase of precipitation is also challenging—the additional water may cause water logging, flooding, and malfunctioning or failure of water-related infrastructure. So the overall risks are growing." Moreover, many industrial produc-

Climate Change Impacts Water Supply

There is now ample evidence that increased hydrologic variability and change in climate has and will continue to have a profound impact on the water sector through the hydrologic cycle, water availability, water demand, and water allocation at the global, regional, basin, and local levels. Many economies are at risk of significant episodic shocks and worsened chronic water scarcity and security. This can have direct and severe ramifications on the economy, poverty, public health and ecosystem viability. . . .

Water practitioners have long coped with and designed for variability in hydrology. Consequently, numerous examples of adaptation to hydrological variability and extreme events exist in the water sector. Implementing the "good practices" more widely (e.g., efficient irrigation technologies, water harvesting, increased subsurface storage, etc.) would go a long way in confronting the climate change challenge. Adapting to climate change must continue to build on conventional interventions while addressing the immediate challenges, but must make a major shift in thinking, planning and designing water investments of the future. New approaches in technology and management, as well as the development of flexible and "smart" systems that can be operated to anticipate and react to changing circumstances must be developed, particularly in light of uncertainties in projected impacts. New design standards and criteria will also need to be developed for a changed hydrology characterized by increased variability and uncertainty.

Vahid Alavian et al., "Water and Climate Change: Understanding the Risks and Making Climate-Smart Investment Decisions," World Bank, December 2009.

tion processes require large amounts of water, so a lack thereof in some regions hampers economic development.

This study is based on a comprehensive set of eleven global hydrological models, forced by five global climate models—a simulation ensemble of unprecedented size which was produced in collaboration by many research groups from around the world. Hence, the findings synthesize the current knowledge about climate change impacts on water availability. The cooperative ISI-MIP process systematically compares the results of the various computer simulations to see where they agree and where they don't. The results quoted above represent the multi-model average. So some of the models indicated even greater increases of water scarcity.

Unique Multi-Model Assessment Allows for Risk Management Perspective

"The multi-model assessment is unique in that it gives us a good measure of uncertainties in future impacts of climate change—which in turn allows us to understand which findings are most robust," says coauthor Pavel Kabat of the International Institute for Applied Systems Analysis (IIASA). "From a risk management perspective, it becomes very clear that, if human-made climate change continues, we are putting at risk the very basis of life for millions of people, even according to the more optimistic scenarios and models."

However, he added, the job is far from being done. "We need to do additional research on how the water requirement portfolio will develop in the future in different sectors like agriculture, industry, and energy—and how, in addition to reducing greenhouse gas emissions, the technological developments in the water sector may help in alleviating water scarcity."

| *"Even without climate change, we are running out of water and I think this has to become the first priority."*

Climate Change Is Not Responsible for Water Scarcity

Pilita Clark

Pilita Clark is an environment correspondent for the Financial Times. *In the following viewpoint, Clark explains that the chairman of Nestlé argues that it is poor water conservation decisions and not global warming that is to blame for water scarcity. Many companies are paying more attention to water conservation, spending more than $84 billion over a three-year period on water conservation and management, according to Clark. Water has become a heated political issue, Clark reports, with environmentalists protesting the actions of companies they believe to be wasting or attempting to privatize water.*

As you read, consider the following questions:

1. How much money has been committed by companies over a three-year period to improve the way they conserve, manage, or obtain water, according to the viewpoint?

2. Why is it wrong to blame global warming for water scarcity, according to Nestlé chairman Peter Brabeck-Letmathe?

3. What evidence does the author cite to back her contention that the politics of water have become volatile?

World leaders must make water scarcity a bigger priority than climate change because the problem is far more urgent than global warming, the chairman of one of the world's biggest food companies has warned.

Water Scarcity Is More Urgent than Climate Change

"Today, you cannot have a political discussion anywhere without talking about climate change," Nestlé chairman Peter Brabeck[-Letmathe] told the *Financial Times* [FT] in an interview. "Nobody talks about the water situation in this sense. And this water problem is much more urgent.

"I am not saying climate change is not important. What I am saying is even without climate change we are running out of water and I think this has to become the first priority," he said, adding that global warming got more attention because it had "better ambassadors" such as Nobel Prize–winning scientists and Hollywood film makers.

Mr Brabeck[-Letmathe]'s comments come as businesses are having to adapt to rising water costs around the world and rivalries mount over poorly managed supplies of a resource long taken for granted.

Companies Are Investing in Water Conservation

In the past three years, companies have committed more than $84bn to improving the way they conserve, manage or obtain water, according to FT research and data from Global Water Intelligence, a market analysis firm.

"Until now, companies have been able to treat water as if it was a free raw material," said Christopher Gasson, Global Water Intelligence's publisher. "Now, the marginal cost of water is rising around the world as governments enforce rules on its use and businesses are discovering they need to invest in equipment to protect everything from their brand to their credit rating."

In the past year alone, BHP Billiton and Rio Tinto, two of the world's biggest miners, agreed to spend $3bn on a desalination plant for a copper mine in Chile, curbing their use of fragile local water supplies.

Nestlé set aside SFr38m ($43m) for water-saving and treatment equipment at its plants around the world while other companies, from the Ford Motor Company to Google, have invested in measures to stem their use of freshwater, an issue Google's data centre head Joe Kava has warned is "the big elephant in the room" for water-hungry data companies.

Coca-Cola and its bottlers have spent nearly $2bn on water conservation measures since 2003, according to the company's head of global water stewardship Greg Koch, including more than $1bn treating discharged wastewater.

"Water scarcity is finally starting to bite financially," said Andrew Metcalf, an investment analyst. In a report last year [2013] for Moody's, the credit rating agency, Mr Metcalf said the problem already had "credit-negative implications" for the mining industry.

Climate change may be playing a role. Energy company EDF spent €20m shifting a water intake tunnel for a hydropower project in the French Alps because the glacier feeding the plant's meltwater had retreated so much the old tunnel no longer worked.

Water Is a Politically Charged Issue

Mr Brabeck[-Letmathe] said it was wrong to blame global warming for water scarcity, however. "We have a water crisis because we make wrong water management decisions," he said, explaining that water was so undervalued it was wasted and overused.

The politics of water have also become volatile. Green groups have criticised Mr Brabeck[-Letmathe] and Nestlé in the past over the company's bottled water business and what activists see as an effort to privatise access to drinking water, a basic human right. Other companies including carmakers, power generators and miners have also faced protests, especially in areas where the world's largest water users—farmers—face tighter supplies.

> *"There is a gigantic warm blob in the Pacific Ocean that is fueling California's four-year-long drought, and it has nothing to do with global warming."*

Climate Change Is Not Responsible for the California Drought

Thomas Richard

Thomas Richard is a Boston-based environmental policy writer. In the following viewpoint, Richard cites two studies that attribute the California drought to natural causes rather than climate change. A study led by Washington State climatologist Nick Bond and a second study led by Dennis Hartmann attribute the drought to a large expanse of water in the Pacific Ocean that is warming the air above. This warm air carries heat rather than rain and snow and is responsible for the four-year drought, Richard reports.

As you read, consider the following questions:

1. What is causing high temperatures and drought conditions on the West Coast of the United States, according to climatologist Nick Bond and his colleagues?

2. According to the viewpoint, what are megaplumes?

3. When did scientists first discover megaplumes, according to Richard?

According to yesterday's [April 10, 2015] *Washington Post*, there is a gigantic warm blob in the Pacific Ocean that is fueling California's four-year-long drought, and it has nothing to do with global warming. Two new studies released this week in the journal *Geophysical Research Letters* explain how this large expanse of warm ocean water is affecting California's weather as well as the East Coast's past two brutal winters.

Natural Causes Are Creating California Drought

In the first study, Nick Bond, Washington's state climatologist, believes the blob, aka the "warm anomaly," is behind California's ongoing warm and dry winters. Discovered in the fall of 2013, the warm anomaly is roughly 1,000 miles wide and about 300 feet deep, and according to Bond, is about 3°C (5°F) warmer than is typical for that area of the Pacific Ocean. When viewed on a map showing ocean water temperatures, "the great circular mass does indeed look like a blob."

Bond and his researchers believe the anomaly was created when a high-pressure air system got stuck over the circular blob's current location, allowing the ocean water to stay calmer and warmer. This in turn allowed the air above this system to carry heat instead of the typical rain and snow as it worked its way toward land, leading to California's multiyear drought.

"The West Coast's high temperatures and dire drought, which has led to mandatory water restrictions in California, are likely attributable to this phenomenon," the researchers said. "These new studies also confirm the National Oceanic and Atmospheric Administration's (NOAA) March report, which said 'that West Coast waters are becoming less biologically productive as they become warmer.' The report attributed the strandings of nearly 1,500 starving sea lion pups, the decline in copepods (tiny crustaceans that support the base of the food chain) and other environmental shifts to the expanding blob." NOAA also put most of the blame on California's drought on natural variables and not climate change.

In the second study, headed by Dennis Hartmann, they found that the "warming waters of the northeast Pacific are tied to an anomaly in water temperatures thousands of miles away, roughly where the international date line and the equator intersect in the tropics." Surface waters in this location are much warmer than normal and are heating the air above them, which eventually reaches the West Coast. Hartmann likens it to "throwing a rock into a pond . . . the wave eventually makes its way to the other side."

And while the warm waters create an unyielding high-pressure system off the West Coast, they cause "cold, wet, low-pressure air in the central and eastern U.S., leading to heavy snowfall and bitterly cold winters." According to the historical record, unusual ocean warming in the tropics has occurred before, and Hartmann admits, "it could be just another natural variation in ocean and atmosphere temperatures, similar to the El Niño–La Niña cycle."

Hartmann declined to say whether the warming of the tropics is due to global warming, writing, "I don't think we know the answer. Maybe it will go away quickly and we won't talk about it anymore, but if it persists for a third year, then we'll know something really unusual is going on." Bond also said in the same joint release that "although the blob does not seem to be caused by climate change, it has many of the same effects for West Coast weather."

The California Drought Is Not a Symptom of Long-Term Climate Change

The current drought is not part of a long-term change in California precipitation, which exhibits no appreciable trend since 1895. Key oceanic features that caused precipitation inhibiting atmospheric ridging off the West Coast during 2011–14 were symptomatic of natural internal atmosphere-ocean variability.

Model simulations indicate that human-induced climate change increases California precipitation in midwinter, with a low-pressure circulation anomaly over the north Pacific, opposite to conditions of the last three winters. The same model simulations indicate a decrease in spring precipitation over California. However, precipitation deficits observed during the past three years are an order of magnitude greater than the model-simulated changes related to human-induced forcing. Nonetheless, record-setting high temperature that accompanied this recent drought was likely made more extreme due to human-induced global warming.

Richard Seager et al.,
"Causes and Predictability of the 2011 to
2014 California Drought," Modeling, Analysis, Predictions
and Projections Program of the Climate Program Office,
NOAA, US Department of Commerce, December 2014.

Megaplumes Impact Climate

The blob also has all the characteristics of another less known phenomena termed megaplumes: massive underwater vents that spew out vast amounts of heat, which in turn warm the waters above. According to geologist James Kamis, "An ongoing very large megaplume is responsible for generating a cell of unusually warm seawater that extends across a vast region of the Pacific Ocean, including much of North America's West Coast. This subsea volcanically induced giant warmed cell is acting to alter normal California climate patterns and inducing a long-term drought."

Even *Discover* magazine noted the importance of a megaplume's influence on ocean waters, writing, "Megaplumes stir up huge amounts of ocean, carrying minerals and gases and heat almost to the sea's surface. Vertical mixing doesn't happen easily in the ocean. Cool, dense water tends to stay near the bottom and warmer buoyant water near the top." David Butterfield, a chemist at the Pacific Marine Environmental Laboratory in Seattle, told *Discover* magazine that, "They could be doing things to the energy of the ocean that we don't even know about."

Scientists first discovered megaplumes in 1986 when they identified a large cell of unusually hot and chemically charged seawater off the coast of Washington State. [Edward T. Baker and colleagues] discovered this phenomenon near the Juan de Fuca Ridge, and it was the first "*cataclysmic* hydrothermal vent or *megaplume*."

NOAA even developed an entire group, the Vents Program, to research hydrothermal vents. "As research by the Vents and other groups progressed, even larger megaplumes were identified," writes Kamis. These include "megaplumes discovered in the Indian and Atlantic Oceans," which were immense: 44 miles by 20 miles by 5,000 feet tall. "Calculations of total energy released per megaplume were so astounding," researchers concluded, that megaplumes could "significantly affect ocean dynamics."

Kamis found that "scientists were beginning to get a handle on the effect that geological forces have on the ocean, and as a result, the climate. Then it happened: Atmospherically trained climate scientists proposed the theory of man-made global warming. Seemingly overnight, these scientists had waylaid further investigation into the megaplumes' effect on the climate."

"Credible evidence increasingly supports the theory of plate climatology, which states that geological forces influence El Niños, Arctic sea ice melt patterns, hydrothermal methane and CO_2 emission rates, deep ocean currents, coral reef bleaching, plankton blooms, mega-droughts, and so on."

"The discovery of geologically induced megaplumes played an important historical role in the evolution of climate science," Kamis adds. "To the satisfaction of field geologists, that notion is currently experiencing a resurrection."

> "While California doesn't necessarily
> need [desalination], a water future
> without it 'would require such severe
> lifestyle changes that I think [desalina-
> tion] is going to be part of the
> equation.'"

California's Last Resort: Drink the Pacific

Sammy Roth

Sammy Roth is energy reporter at Desert Sun Media Group. In the following viewpoint, Roth argues that although desalination is expensive, uses a great deal of energy, contributes to climate change, and may harm marine life, it is the best solution available for water-deprived regions such as California, Israel, and Saudi Arabia. Roth reports that city officials in Santa Barbara, CA, consider the desalination plant scheduled to open in late 2016 as a last resort necessary to combat drought. Critics of desalination worry that it will create a false sense of security that will discourage water conservation and efficiencies, the reporter states. However, desalination supporters say that the lifestyle changes without desalination would be too drastic for people to accept, Roth concludes.

As you read, consider the following questions:

1. According to Roth, how much will the desalination plant being built in Santa Barbara cost?

2. What are some of the problems with desalination, according to the viewpoint?

3. According to Santa Barbara's water resources manager, how much does the city pay for surface water, groundwater, and recycled water, and what does he estimate desalinated water will cost?

You can't see the desalination plant from the beach in Santa Barbara. It's a few blocks from the ocean, tucked between a sewage treatment center and the Pacific Coast Highway, and in any case it's not very big. Just a row of water tanks, a few powerful pumps, some office space and a mess of pipes.

For nearly 25 years, the desal plant has sat unused. That's about to change.

No Other Choice

As nearby beachgoers swam, sailed and paddleboarded on an overcast morning last week [in April 2015], Santa Barbara officials showed off those tanks and pumps, describing their plan to turn seawater into drinking water. It'll be expensive: up to $40 million to bring the desal plant back online, plus $5 million per year to keep it running. Water bills are expected to increase by about $20 per month. And for all that money, the city will meet 30 percent of its water needs at best.

City officials say the drought has left them with no other choice.

"With a drought of this nature, there isn't really any water supply that's going to help us aside from desalination," said Joshua Haggmark, Santa Barbara's water resources manager. "For the time being, this is our supply of last resort."

Desalination is a simple concept: Pump water from the ocean, remove the salt and drink. Water-poor countries like Israel and Saudi Arabia rely heavily on desal, and as California's historic drought drags on, the promise of a nearly unlimited water supply lapping at our shores is increasingly tempting to many water districts.

As desalination's many critics will tell you, it's a lot harder in practice than it is in theory. For one thing, it's extremely expensive, as Santa Barbara residents will soon discover. It also uses massive amounts of energy, which can exacerbate climate change, and it's dangerous for marine life if not done carefully.

But despite those concerns, it's starting to become inevitable that California will get more of its water from the Pacific Ocean.

State officials are evaluating 15 proposed plants, from the Bay Area to Camp Pendleton in San Diego County. The largest desal plant in the Western Hemisphere will come online in Carlsbad later this year, providing water for 300,000 people in San Diego County at a cost of approximately $1 billion. Another plant proposed for Huntington Beach would be just as big.

Advocates tout desalination as a drought-proof water source. They argue that as California's population grows, and as climate change makes droughts more frequent and more severe, we'll need desalinated water more than ever.

"Obviously we've done tons in conservation, but we have to have enough water," said Sandy Kerl, deputy general manager of the San Diego County Water Authority, which is buying the water from the Carlsbad desal plant. "You have to have some base level of water. You can't conserve what you don't have."

Even desal's critics say the technology is likely to play a role in California's water future—eventually. For them, the question isn't whether the technology makes sense—it's whether it makes sense to start using it now, when there are so many cheaper, safer strategies for meeting our water needs. Those strategies include conservation and wastewater recycling.

"We really need to ask ourselves, what else could we be doing at lower cost?" said Heather Cooley, water program director for the Pacific Institute, an Oakland-based research organization. "We have to look at it within that sort of context, and see if there are options that provide the same benefits, but with fewer social and environmental costs."

High Cost, High Reward

This isn't the first time California has suffered from critical water shortages. Faced with a then record-breaking drought in the early 1990s, Santa Barbara commissioned the state's largest seawater desalination plant, which produced nearly 6.7 million gallons per day.

But by the time the desal plant was finished, the drought was ending. As rain blanketed the state, Santa Barbara suddenly had easy access to cheap water, and it shut down the $35 million facility after just three months.

The city's experience mirrors that of Australia, where officials poured billions of dollars into six enormous desalination plants during the "millennium drought" that started in the mid-1990s. By the late 2000s, when those plants started to come online, it seemed like the drought might never end.

But then it did, washed away by a series of torrential rains in 2010. Four of the continent's massive desal plants now sit idle, according to Sandra Kentish, a chemical engineering professor and desalination expert at the University of Melbourne.

"Virtually the day that we commissioned those, it rained heavily across most of the eastern part of Australia," Kentish said. "There has been a lot of controversy here about whether those plants should have been built."

Critics call Australia's experience a cautionary tale about the dangers of sinking money into desalination plants you don't absolutely need. They worry the same thing will happen in California, with taxpayers footing the bill for billions of dollars' worth of desal facilities that could shut down once the drought ends.

Advocates, though, see desalination as part of a longer-term solution to California's unsustainable water use. Climate change, they point out, is likely to result in more frequent and more severe droughts, and some scientists believe decades-long could become increasingly common in the western United States. The state's population, which has more than doubled over the last half century, will continue to rise.

The Carlsbad plant was first proposed in 1998, long before the current drought. The San Diego County Water Authority has been trying for years to diversify its water sources and reduce its reliance on imported water, and it sees the Carlsbad project as a natural step in that direction.

"Drought is a common thing. We didn't propose this plant as a knee-jerk reaction to the drought that is happening right now," said Jessica Jones, a spokesperson for Poseidon Water, which is building the Carlsbad plant. "Regardless of whether the drought continues, there is a need for water in California."

Santa Barbara officials expect their long-shuttered desal plant to reopen in late 2016. City policy makers haven't discussed whether to keep it running when the drought ends—or whether to use it at all, if the drought ends before next year—but Mayor Helene Schneider said it's a conversation they need to have.

"We know that one day this drought will end. We also know there'll be another drought in the future," she said. "So instead of going through this panic mode of reauthorizing and restructuring a desalination plant, should we think differently in terms of, 'Should desal be a part of a regular water supply for the region, even at a small level, when we're not in a drought?'"

The answer to that question could be determined by the shifting costs of obtaining water. Desalination has been getting cheaper as technology improves, and in California, importing water has been getting more expensive as supplies dwindle.

Haggmark, Santa Barbara's water resources manager, said the city pays about $300 per acre-foot of surface water, $800 per acre-foot of groundwater, and $1,200 per acre-foot of recycled water. He expects desalinated water to cost between $1,300 and $1,500 per acre-foot—more expensive than other sources, but relatively close to recycled water.

San Diego County's desalinated water will be more expensive, costing about $2,000 per acre-foot and likely causing a $5 to $7 spike in average monthly water bills.

Officials in San Diego County and Santa Barbara say they aren't expecting a major backlash to higher water costs. But even in Australia—where the high costs of desalination have generated the most controversy—it's not yet clear whether the investment will pay off.

"My own feeling is that we will use (the desal plants). It's only a matter of time," Kentish said. "I still think it's a good investment, because of climate change."

Water and Energy

The process for turning ocean water into drinking water is relatively simple.

Seawater is pumped into desal facilities through intake pipes snaking out into the ocean, before being filtered for sediment and other large solids. Usually, the water is then forced through special membranes in a process called reverse osmosis, removing the dissolved salt. Finally, the salty water that didn't make it through the membranes is dumped back into the ocean.

It's the high-pressure reverse osmosis step that requires enormous amounts of energy. In order to supply water to 300,000 people, the Carlsbad desal plant will require the equivalent of a 31.3 megawatt power plant operating around the clock—enough electricity to power nearly 40,000 average California households for a year.

Unsurprisingly, desalination is the most energy-intensive method of obtaining water in California, according to a 2013 report from the Pacific Institute. It uses more energy per gallon than even the [California] State Water Project, a complex system of aqueducts that pumps water from the state's wet northern regions to its parched south.

That energy consumption is a big reason desal is so expensive. It's also an environmental red flag, as desal's critics are quick to point out. As long as California gets most of its electricity from burning fossil fuels—*which it does*—energy-intensive processes like desalination will contribute to climate change, exacerbating the water shortages that desal is supposed to help alleviate.

Desalination "keeps us moving in this cycle," said Matt O'Malley of San Diego Coastkeeper, which has opposed the Carlsbad desal plant. "We really need to get out of this water-energy cycle."

No one desal plant will have a noticeable impact on the climate. But if California goes all in on desalination, approving the 15 plants that have been proposed, desal could have a "pretty significant" impact on the state's overall electricity use, said Kelly Sanders, an engineering professor at the University of Southern California who has studied the energy-water nexus.

Desalination Works in Israel

As California and other western areas of the United States grapple with an extreme drought, a revolution has taken place [in Israel]. A major national effort to desalinate Mediterranean seawater and to recycle wastewater has provided the country with enough water for all its needs, even during severe droughts. More than 50 percent of the water for Israeli households, agriculture and industry is now artificially produced.

Isabel Kershner,
"Aided by the Sea, Israel Overcomes an Old Foe: Drought,"
New York Times, *May 29, 2015.*

Even without widespread desalination, she noted, water accounts for a small but not insignificant slice of California's energy use. The State Water Project alone uses 2 to 3 percent of all electricity consumed in California, according to the U.S. Environmental Protection Agency.

"I think the drought is making a lot of people nervous, and it's very important that we plan for it," Sanders said. "At the same time, I think there's other modes of water conservation and water supply we could move to before really making desal available on the large scale."

Desal advocates note that the technology has become more energy efficient over time, and that it's likely to keep moving in that direction. Poseidon Water, meanwhile, has said it will study the feasibility of generating solar energy at the Carlsbad plant. Poseidon will fund projects that pull carbon from the atmosphere, offsetting the desal plant's energy-related greenhouse gas emissions.

Environmental Impacts

Energy use isn't the only environmental problem with desalination. Pumping ocean water can kill marine life small enough to get through intake filters, and dumping desalination's extremely salty leftovers back in the ocean can prove similarly fatal.

In Santa Barbara, officials plan to install new intake screens with 1 millimeter openings, which should keep out most species. But fish eggs and larvae at the bottom of the food chain will still be sucked into the pipes, and local environmental groups fear ripple effects that could affect a wide range of species.

"We have a very rich fishing industry here in Santa Barbara, and the impacts to that are what we're mostly concerned about," said Kira Redmond, executive director of Santa Barbara Channelkeeper.

Santa Barbara plans to contribute $500,000 to projects that support small marine life. Poseidon Water, meanwhile, will fund wetland restoration projects that benefit marine species and ecosystems.

But for environmental groups, those kinds of projects are a sorry excuse for mitigation.

"Trying to make up for a lot of death somewhere else is not really mitigation," O'Malley said. "You want to cut down on that mortality in the first place."

The best way to do that, environmentalists say, is to build intake pipes beneath the ocean floor, using the sand as a natural filter to keep out marine life. Building "subsurface" intake pipes isn't physically possible along some parts of California's coast, but where possible, it should be the default, proponents say.

Subsurface pipes are more expensive than traditional "open ocean" pipes, but they're likely to become the norm in California. The State Water Resources Control Board is set to vote next month on new guidelines that would require regional water boards to determine whether subsurface intakes are feasible before approving desal plants with open ocean intakes.

Still, the new guidelines won't affect desal plants that have already been approved, including those in Santa Barbara and Carlsbad. Both plants will use open ocean intakes, although Santa Barbara plans to study the feasibility of subsurface intakes.

Desal's other environmental challenge is how to dispose of the salt. For every gallon of clean drinking water that a desal plant produces, there's as much as a gallon of salty water that must be returned to the ocean, even though it now has a far higher salt concentration than seawater—potentially deadly for many species.

In Santa Barbara, environmental advocates aren't too concerned about the brine, because the city plans to mix it with less salty water from a wastewater treatment plant before returning it to the ocean. And the state water board's new desal guidelines will force all plants to dump their brine in a less harmful way than is currently required.

But even with stricter rules, desal won't become a silver bullet for solving California's water woes, said Claire Waggoner, an environmental scientist at the state water board who has worked on the new guidelines. While desalination "makes your water pie a little bit bigger," Waggoner noted, even the Western Hemisphere's largest desal plant will meet just 7 percent of San Diego County's water needs.

"It's a tool. If a water developer wants to use it, these are the rules that you should have. But we shouldn't be putting all our eggs in one basket," Waggoner said. "We're in such dire straits with the drought, we need to explore everything."

Last Resort

Even desalination's harshest critics say they aren't opposed to it entirely. The debate in California is centered on questions like when we should turn to desal and how much water we should desalinate—and whether desalination makes any sense as a drought solution.

Desal's critics call the technology a distraction from cheaper, safer drought solutions, including conservation, efficiency, wastewater recycling and storm water capture.

There's no question that Californians could be doing a lot more to save water, considering we haven't come close to meeting the 20 percent reduction target that Gov. Jerry Brown set last year. Brown announced mandatory 25 percent water cuts earlier this month, and some areas—including much of the Coachella Valley—will be required to reduce their water use by 35 percent.

"Really, the fundamental problem with (desal) is it doesn't force people to think differently about water," Redmond said. "And that's what we really need in California, is a cultural shift in the way we think about water, where we get it and how we use it. We need to understand, we don't need green lawns."

Advocates say it's never been their intention to portray desalination as an all-encompassing drought solution, and that conservation is critical with or without the technology. In Santa Barbara and San Diego County, officials say that even with further water cutbacks, they'll still need seawater to help meet their needs.

But for critics, it's hard not to see desal as a deceptively simple solution to an incredibly difficult problem. Policy makers and water users might be tempted to slack off on conservation and efficiency if the state moves too quickly to adopt desalination, they argue.

"There is a real concern that by building desalination plants, it does reduce pressure to develop cheaper options," Cooley said.

Even if Californians reduce their water use by 25 percent, though, it's still likely that more desal plants will be built—at some point. Sanders believes that while California doesn't necessarily need desal, a water future without it "would require such severe lifestyle changes that I think desal is going to be part of the equation."

> "The world needs to address its water problems, and currently conservation—not desalination—appears to be the best course."

Desalination Is Not the Answer to the Global Water Crisis

Aaron Lada

Aaron Lada is a writer for EcoHearth.com. In the following viewpoint, Lada maintains that although there is a worldwide shortage of clean water that will only get worse in the future, water conservation, not desalination, is the answer. One major problem with desalination is its cost; desalination is typically two to four times as expensive as treating freshwater, he explains. Lada goes on to say that there are also significant environmental issues with desalination, including an increase in greenhouse gas emissions and the potential for contaminating groundwater.

As you read, consider the following questions:

1. According to the viewpoint, what percentage of the earth's water is available for use?

2. What are the two main approaches to desalination, according to Lada?

3. According to Lada, why is desalination so expensive?

The success of any human settlement hinges on the availability of freshwater. Due to a variety of factors, many areas are experiencing water shortages that threaten to become more widespread. Desalination, the process of removing salt from seawater, is capable of providing freshwater to arid locations. Yet its exorbitant cost and potential for environmental harm currently prevent exploitation of this technology. Is there hope that desalination will be the answer to the world's water problems?

A Worsening Water Crisis

Less than 1% of the earth's water is fresh and available for use. Our poor stewardship of water resources has caused even this scant supply to dwindle, while at the same time demand is rising. Indeed, global water consumption is doubling every 20 years, and projections estimate that *by 2025, demand for water will exceed the supply by 56%.* Factors such as population growth, climate change, and increased demand by industry and agriculture have made water a valuable resource that often dictates financial and security issues. Thus tapping into the saltwater of the oceans—which cover more than two-thirds of the planet's surface—as a source for freshwater appears to be an attractive solution.

How It Works

There are two main approaches to desalination: distillation and membrane filtration. Based on methods used for thousands of years, distillation involves boiling seawater to produce steam—purified water vapor. The steam is collected in a separate container and cooled so it will condense back into water.

Newer technologies such as reverse osmosis and electrodialysis use filters to desalinate water. In reverse osmosis, the filter permits water to cross while excluding salt. Pressure is applied to a tank of seawater forcing water through the membrane; the desalinated water is collected on the other side.

Electrodialysis uses an electric current instead of pressure, and salt can move across its filter. The current induces a charge on the salt molecules, and electrodes holding the opposite charge are placed on the other side of the membrane. Attraction to the electrodes pulls the salt across, leaving purified water behind.

Desalination plants are located near an ocean and use large pipes to bring in the water, which is first pretreated to remove particulate matter, kill pathogens and bring it to the appropriate pH [a measure of the acidity or alkalinity of a substance]. All desalination methods produce a concentrated waste product composed of the salts found in seawater and chemicals used in the process. Disposal methods for the concentrate include dumping it back in the ocean, injecting it into deep underground wells, storing it in above-ground evaporation ponds, and zero-liquid discharge procedures that produce a solid waste product.

Associated Costs

All the current desalination methods require large amounts of energy, with distillation being the most energy intensive. This makes desalination very expensive, with approximately 20–35% of the price due to energy costs. Generally, desalination is two to four times as expensive as treating freshwater, but this varies by location based on the quality of water treated, method used and types of energy available. Desalination is sometimes the only choice for producing potable water in desert and arid regions, and while wealthy countries can afford the cost, it isn't yet an option in poorer areas.

One way to reduce the cost is to treat brackish water—groundwater with a much lower salt content than seawater. Since there is less salt to remove, less energy is required.

Another cost-saving measure is to locate desalination plants together with thermoelectric power plants that use seawater to cool their generators. The power plant would preheat the seawater that could then be desalinated at a lower cost, since less energy would be needed.

Environmental Issues with Desalination

There are several ways in which desalination can harm the environment. But even treatment and overuse of freshwater can negatively impact ecosystems—including draining lakes dry and preventing rivers from reaching their final destinations.

Specific concerns [of desalination]:

- Large amounts of energy are required and if fossil fuels are used, it increases greenhouse gas emissions.

- Disposing of the concentrate back into the ocean can harm organisms and disrupt ecosystems. Other disposal methods haven't yet been proven as safe alternatives.

- Aquatic organisms are killed while pumping in seawater.

- Building a large desalination facility impacts the local ecology.

- More people might be attracted to move to fragile coastal areas if a reliable source of water is available.

- Seawater intake pipes could leak and contaminate groundwater.

The Future of Desalination

Currently, there are more than 12,000 desalination plants in 120 countries producing less than 1% of freshwater consumed globally. Yet, according to a Natural Resources Defense Council report desalination isn't the answer to water shortage issues caused by climate change. In fact, the report concludes that *water conservation methods would be more effective* at addressing shortages than desalination.

But desalination technology is improving; in the last ten years advances in reverse osmosis have led to significant energy reductions. The concept of biomimicry, which uses designs and techniques found in nature to solve modern problems, has led to new reverse osmosis filters that take cues from how individual cells move water across their membranes. Water can either move directly across the cell membrane or pass through protein channels called aquaporins. It is more efficient for water to cross through an aquaporin, and an internal positive charge repels salts, making them selective. A company, aptly named Aquaporin, is developing membranes with similarly designed selective channels that allow water to cross the membrane more easily, requiring less pressure and thus less energy.

As long as the global population and temperature continue to increase, water shortages will become more common. Desalination can effectively produce freshwater, but its high price and potential to harm the environment have kept it from becoming a major supplier. The world needs to address its water problems, and currently conservation—not desalination—appears to be the best course.

Periodical and Internet Sources Bibliography

The following articles have been selected to supplement the diverse views presented in this chapter.

Kieran Cooke	"Worsening Water Scarcity to Affect 2 Billion Globally," Climate Central, September 21, 2013.
Dennis Dimick	"If You Think the Water Crisis Can't Get Worse, Wait Until the Aquifers Are Drained," *National Geographic*, August 21, 2014.
Chris Edwards	"California, Drought, and Water Policy," Cato Institute, June 27, 2014.
Natasha Geiling	"Why Food Companies Aren't Prepared to Deal with Water Scarcity," *ClimateProgress*, May 9, 2015.
Barbara Grady	"Most Food Companies Ignore the Risks of Water Scarcity," *GreenBiz*, May 8, 2015.
Brandon Griggs	"How Oceans Can Solve Our Freshwater Crisis," CNN, May 26, 2014.
Alyssa Martino	"Water Scarcity Is Helping Radicalize the Middle East," *Vice*, April 25, 2015.
Robin McKie	"Why Fresh Water Shortages Will Cause the Next Great Global Crisis," *Guardian*, March 7, 2015.
Steve Scauzillo	"Can Waste-Water Recycling, Desalination End California's Water Wars?," *San Gabriel Valley Tribune*, June 30, 2015.
Quirin Schiermeier	"Water Risk as World Warms," *Nature*, December 31, 2013.
Kevin D. Williamson	"The Dry Math of Scarcity," *National Review Online*, April 8, 2015.

Does Social Equity Promote Global Sustainability?

Chapter Preface

The three pillars of sustainable development are economic development, social equity, and environmental protection. Of the three, the concept of social equity has been the most elusive to define and has received less attention than environmental issues. However, it is the position of the United Nations (UN) that true sustainability requires the convergence of all three pillars.

In his highly anticipated encyclical *Laudato si'*, Pope Francis brought the issue of social equity to the forefront in his words about the role climate change plays in deepening the divide between the haves and have-nots of the world. Although poverty-stricken individuals are not mainly responsible for the carbon emissions that are destabilizing the environment, they are the ones who will suffer the most from it. The pope argued:

> Inequity affects not only individuals but entire countries; it compels us to consider an ethics of international relations. A true 'ecological debt' exists, particularly between the global north and south, connected to commercial imbalances with effects on the environment, and the disproportionate use of natural resources by certain countries over long periods of time. . . . The warming caused by huge consumption on the part of some rich countries has repercussions on the poorest areas of the world, especially Africa, where a rise in temperature, together with drought, has proved devastating for farming.

Environmentalists enthusiastically hailed the encyclical. The United Nations quickly released a statement by Secretary-General Ban Ki-moon supporting the encyclical. Additionally, Jim Yong Kim, president of the World Bank, called the pope's encyclical a "stark reminder" of the link between poverty and climate change, saying, "The impacts of climate change, in-

137

cluding the increased frequency of extreme weather events, are most devastating for the unacceptably high number of people today living in extreme poverty."

Climate change skeptics were not enthusiastic. Even before the encyclical's release, Dennis Prager writing at Townhall.com said, "Any Catholic who tweets, 'Inequality is the root of social evil,' as Pope Francis did last March, should be a socialist prime minister, not a Christian leader. The moral message of every Bible-based religion is that the root of evil is caused by poor character and poor moral choices, not by economics."

Following the release of the encyclical, Jim Lakely, director of communications for the Heartland Institute, said, "Pope Francis's heart is in the right place, but he made a grave mistake by putting his trust and moral authority behind agenda-driven bureaucrats at the United Nations who have been bearing false witness about the causes and consequences of climate change for decades."

The differing views presented in the following chapter are emblematic of the controversies surrounding the issue of social equity with scientists, commentators, and journalists debating whether social equity promotes global sustainability.

"Put simply, we're all in this together economically, socially, and environmentally."

Social Equity Is Necessary for Global Sustainability

James H. Svara, Tanya Watt, and Katherine Takai

James H. Svara is a research professor at the School of Public Affairs at Arizona State University and a visiting professor at the School of Government at the University of North Carolina at Chapel Hill. Tanya Watt is an instructor and graduate research assistant at Arizona State University. Katherine Takai is a project manager at the Center for Sustainable Communities of the International City/County Management Association (ICMA). In the following viewpoint, Svara, Watt, and Takai summarize the results of a survey on local government sustainability policies and programs conducted by the ICMA. The survey found that while most local governments had programs encompassing such issues as recycling, the environment, and energy conservation, fewer than one in ten were adequately addressing social equity.

James H. Svara, Tanya Watt, and Katherine Takai, "Local Governments, Social Equity, and Sustainable Communities: Advancing Social Equity Goals to Achieve Sustainability," Washington, DC: US Department of Housing and Urban Development, October 1, 2014. Copyright © 2014 by International City/County Management Association (ICMA). All rights reserved. Reproduced with permission.

In order for communities to remain viable, they must put in place measures to address past inequities and prevent them from occurring in the future, the researchers contend. The work that provided the basis for this publication was supported by funding under a grant with the US Department of Housing and Urban Development. The substance and findings of the work are dedicated to the public. The author and publisher are solely responsible for the accuracy of the statements and interpretations contained in this publication. Such interpretations do not necessarily reflect the views of the government.

As you read, consider the following questions:

1. What is the purpose of social equity, according to the authors?

2. What are some of the benefits of social equity, according to the viewpoint?

3. According to the viewpoint, what percentage of the local governments responding to the ICMA survey were active in social equity?

Since the 1980s, sustainability—defined as measures taken to protect and enhance the environment, the economy, and equity for current residents and future generations—has become an issue of increasing importance both domestically and internationally. In the past decade, local governments have demonstrated increasing leadership in this area. Some exemplary local government officials have worked in partnership with businesses, nonprofits, community organizations, and residents to collaboratively develop programs to create more vibrant, resilient communities.

Social Equity Is Addressed by Few Local Governments

In 2010, ICMA [International City/County Management Association] conducted its local government sustainability policies and programs survey and found that most local governments were still in the early stages of addressing sustainability. Most placed emphasis on long-standing areas of commitment such as recycling and the environment as well as on new areas such as energy conservation, but only a minority of governments had developed comprehensive sustainability programs. Few were adopting measures to promote social equity.

Without a strong commitment to social equity, local governments have moved only part of the way toward achieving true sustainability. The experience of American urban areas shows that inequality and social exclusion are not sustainable practices because they undermine the viability of communities. Thus communities might have programs that protect the natural environment, reduce energy use, and address other aspects of sustainability, but without programs to promote social equity, they are not strengthening their social foundation for long-term viability.

This research examines the extent to which social equity activities are included within an integrated approach to sustainability, how social equity is defined, and the level of commitment of local governments in addressing equity issues. Social equity means redressing injustices and remediating damages that were previously incurred, fully incorporating all segments of the community in the political process, and establishing measures to prevent future inequities from occurring. Such efforts include expanding opportunity and promoting equal access to public services; providing equal service quality; ensuring procedural fairness; and striving for equal opportunity in such areas as education, health, and employment. The social equity dimension of sustainability refers to how burdens and benefits of different policy actions are distributed in a community. The more evenly they are distributed, the more equitable the community is, and this is reflected in economic, ecologic, and social outcomes.

The United States Is Becoming More Socially Stratified

It's a puzzle: One dispossessed group after another—blacks, women, Hispanics and gays—has been gradually accepted in the United States, granted equal rights and brought into the mainstream.

At the same time, in economic terms, the United States has gone from being a comparatively egalitarian society to one of the most unequal democracies in the world.

The two shifts are each huge and hugely important: One shows a steady march toward democratic inclusion, the other toward a tolerance of economic stratification that would have been unthinkable a generation ago.

Alexander Stille, "The Paradox of the New Elite,"
New York Times, *October 22, 2011.*

This [viewpoint] describes the current activities, leading practices, and achievements of sustainable communities. Such communities were created through a comprehensive, integrated approach to sustainability supported by inclusive engagement, equal access to services, and livable neighborhoods. The analysis examines all local governments that responded to the ICMA 2010 survey, focusing in particular on the characteristics of the minority of governments—fewer than 1 in 10—that are very active in social equity. Using additional information from a follow-up survey conducted in 2012, the analysis explores the adoption of a wider range of equity activities. From these surveys, nine local governments were identified for in-depth examination as case studies.

Key Observations from Case Studies

1. Inclusive citizen engagement has played a critical role in improving the quality of public projects, improving relationships between the public and city government, and increasing the overall quality of life for community residents.

2. Formal and informal networks of service providers and stakeholders are needed to advance social equity goals.

3. Clearly articulating the importance of social equity in local government mobilizes support and resources.

4. A holistic approach to comprehensively serving the needs of the most marginalized groups in a community is critical to achieving social equity.

5. In local governments that are truly pursuing a holistic approach to sustainability, sustainability activities are dispersed throughout a number of departments in local governments. Formal sustainability offices rarely encapsulate all sustainability activities undertaken by the local government as a whole.

6. There are a number of organizing themes by which the objectives of sustainability and social equity can be achieved. In cases where there is a tradition of supporting other goals or where sustainability, climate change, or equity is a particularly politically sensitive topic, other organizing strategies can be successful in achieving desired outcomes.

7. Local governments can encourage the acceptance of certain initiatives (for example, affordable housing or housing that is universally accessible, green building, or an increased number of healthy food outlets in the community) by well-designed incentives that avoid unintended barriers to desired projects.

8. Targeted outreach and assistance are required to involve low-income households in energy conservation projects and other sustainability projects, thereby extending the benefits of these programs to persons in need.

9. The support of elected leadership for sustainability and social equity initiatives is crucial for the long-term commitment necessary to achieve positive results. In the absence of such leadership, resources may be redistributed to address other priorities, thereby diminishing the positive impact that sustainability programs might otherwise achieve.

10. Leadership on social equity–related initiatives can come from staff members in all areas of local government, and social service–oriented staff is required for success. Such initiatives can be pursued laterally and vertically.

11. Restoring the physical assets of the past in the downtown and neighborhoods to preserve history and cultural traditions provides a foundation for revitalization and new development in distressed neighborhoods.

12. Current performance metrics in social equity leave a considerable amount to be desired, and measures that integrate social equity with environmental and economic indicators in sustainability plans are often largely absent. Public health seems to be the area of social equity in which indicators are most developed.

Many communities (both surveyed and selected for case study) have an extensive range of sustainability activities, such as affordable housing programs, wellness initiatives, preschool programs, and actions to promote job creation. However, surprisingly few of these governments are organizing and resourcing their sustainability initiatives in a coordinated manner or through a comprehensive plan. Fewer still are addressing social equity issues as an integrated part of their sustainability strategies. From these observations, a few key recommendations may include the following:

- It is important to get local governments that are overall leaders in sustainability more involved in social equity, as they have a lot of sustainability experience to build on and some supportive policy priorities.

- Local governments with leading practices in sustainability and social equity can serve as examples to other governments that have not yet made a substantial commitment to social equity or even to sustainability.

- Much progress can be achieved by moving the majority of local governments from below-average to average levels of activity in sustainability overall and in social equity. . . .

The key point for promoting social equity activities is that exclusion and inequality are not sustainable practices. Put simply, we're all in this together economically, socially, and environmentally. If we want livable and viable communities, we must pursue a comprehensive approach to sustainability that includes social equity.

> *"The true purpose of sustainable development and all of its policies is the control of all aspects of human life—economic, social and environmental."*

Social Equity Leads to the Loss of Individual Rights

Kathleen Marquardt

Kathleen Marquardt is the founder and former chairman of Putting People First. She is a contributing writer and researcher for Freedom Advocates and the author of AnimalScam: The Beastly Abuse of Human Rights. *In the following viewpoint, Marquardt sharply criticizes the principles of Agenda 21, the action plan for global sustainability developed during the Earth Summit in Rio de Janeiro, Brazil, in 1992. She contends that Agenda 21 is an assault on the US Constitution and threatens private property and the rights of the individual. Proponents of sustainable development say the steps outlined in Agenda 21 are necessary to protect the environment, but their real goal is to control every aspect of human life and to redistribute wealth, Marquardt says.*

As you read, consider the following questions:

1. According to Marquardt, what is "newspeak"?

2. What does Agenda 21 mean by "social justice," according to Marquardt?

3. According to the viewpoint, what are the three Es of sustainability?

In simple terms, Agenda 21 is the end of civilization as we know it. It is the end of private property, the elevation of the collective over the individual. It is the redistribution of America's wealth to the global elite; it is the end of the Great American Experiment and the Constitution. And, it is the reduction of 85% of the world's population.

Birth of an Abomination

In 1992, twenty years ago this summer, Agenda 21 was unveiled to the world at the UN's [United Nations'] Earth Summit in Rio. (While Agenda 21 was introduced in June 1992, it was already installed as public policy in communities across the country as early as 1987.)

In his opening remarks at the ceremonies at the Earth Summit, Maurice Strong stated: "The concept of national sovereignty has been an immutable, indeed sacred, principle of international relations. It is a principle which will yield only slowly and reluctantly to the new imperatives of global environmental cooperation. It is simply not feasible for sovereignty to be exercised unilaterally by individual nation-states, however powerful. The global community must be assured of environmental security." If this is true, then he and his cohorts must be even more against individual sovereignty. Keep this quote in mind as you read about Agenda 21.

George H.W. Bush was in Rio for the ceremonies and graciously signed on for America so that our Congress did not have to spend the time reviewing the treaty and learning then what dastardly deeds were in store for us—that protecting the environment would be used as the basis for controlling all human activity and redistributing our wealth.

Definitions of Sustainable Development

UN definition of sustainable development:

> "meeting today's needs without compromising future generations to meet their own needs."

In actuality, sustainable development is not sustainable unless the population actually is reduced by the 85% called for by the globalists. The true purpose of sustainable development and all of its policies is the control of all aspects of human life—economic, social and environmental. . . .

Here is how the UN described Agenda 21 in one of its own publications in a 1993 article entitled "Agenda 21: The Earth Summit Strategy to Save Our Planet":

> "Agenda 21 proposes an array of actions which are intended to be implemented by EVERY person on Earth . . . it calls for specific changes in the activities of ALL people. . . . Effective execution of Agenda 21 will REQUIRE a profound reorientation of ALL humans, unlike anything the world has ever experienced."

So George H.W. Bush signed the Rio accord and a year later [Bill] Clinton established his President's Council on Sustainable Development, which would render the guidelines of Agenda 21 into public policy to be administered by the federal government via all departments. In doing this, Bush and Clinton set up Agenda 21 as ruling authority, i.e., implementing a UN plan to become U.S. policy across the whole nation and into every county and town. And every succeeding president has fully endorsed and implemented Agenda 21 through every department of the federal government.

If one were to research the source of U.S. policy, one would find that much of our policy of the last few decades is the outcome of agreements we have entered into via treaties with the UN. And that policy has trickled, no gushed, down into every state and into almost every other jurisdiction—county, city, town—in the nation; sustainable development is the official policy of our country, even though many citizens are yet ignorant of its existence. And this policy encompasses an entire economic and social agenda.

So What Is Sustainable Development?

According to its authors, the objective of sustainable development is to integrate economic, social and environmental policies in order to achieve reduced consumption, social equity, and the preservation and restoration of biodiversity (the 3 Es of sustainability). They insist that every societal decision be based on environmental impact, focusing on three components: global land use, global education, and global population control and reduction.

Look at these words, they are part of the new vocabulary:

Free trade, open space, smart growth, smart food, smart buildings, regional planning, walkable, bikeable, food sheds, view sheds, consensus, partnerships, preservation, stakeholders, land use, environmental protection, development, diversity, visioning, social justice, heritage, carbon footprints, comprehensive planning, critical thinking, community service, regional planning.

All of these words are part of the newspeak, the altering of the English language as a tool to promote a global government through a diabolical agenda called Agenda 21. In fact, the world will be retooled from top to bottom through this agenda and using the new vocabulary. This is not just policy but a complete restructuring of life as we know it. We not only will be taught how we must live, but where we are allowed to live; taught how to think and what is acceptable thinking; told what job we will be allowed to have; taught how we can worship and what we will be allowed to worship;

and we will be brainwashed into believing that the individual must cede all to the collective.

Private property will be a sin that will be eradicated as will be free market economics, which will be replaced by public-private partnerships and a planned central economy. Individualism will be rooted out and social justice will rule the land. Social justice is described as the right and opportunity of all people "*to benefit equally from the resources afforded us by society and the environment*"—in other words, the redistribution of wealth. This will be achieved through an organizational structure of land use controls; control of energy and energy production; control of transportation; control of industry; control of food production; control of development; control of water availability; and control of population size and growth. And all of this will be decreed under the guise of environmental protection.

The 3 Es of sustainability, which make up the sustainable development logo, consists of three connecting circles labeled social equity; economic prosperity; and ecological integrity. These Es together encompass every aspect of human life.

First E—Social Equity

Social equity is based on a demand for "social justice"—in non-newspeak, redistribution of the wealth.

Social justice is described as the right and opportunity of all people "to benefit equally from the resources afforded us by society and the environment." Redistribution of wealth. Private property is a social injustice since not everyone can build wealth from it. National sovereignty is a social injustice. Universal health care is a social injustice. . . .

Equity is a system of "social justice" that works to abolish the American concept of equal justice in order to pursue the globalist ideal of the "common good." Individual rights must be abolished for the good of the collective, just as in communism; in fact, Karl Marx was the first person to use the term

Agenda 21 Is Against America's Founding Principles

We who oppose [Agenda 21] don't believe that the world is in such dire emergency environmentally that we must destroy the very human civilization that brought us from a life of nothing but survival against the elements into a world that gave us homes, health care, food, and even luxury. Sustainable development advocates literally hope to roll back our civilization to the days of mere survival and we say NO. Why should we? We have found great deception in the promotion of the global warming argument. We believe in free markets and free societies where people make their own decisions, live and develop their own property. And we fully believe that the true path to a strong protection of the environment is through private property ownership and limited government. Those who promote Agenda 21 do not believe in those ideals. And so we will not agree on the path to the future. And our fight is just that—a clash of philosophy. There is very little room for middle ground.

The United States has never been part of a global village in which rules for life have been handed down by some self-appointed village elders. We are a nation of laws that were designed to protect our right to our property and our individual life choices while keeping government reined in. We oppose Agenda 21 precisely because it represents the exact opposite view of government.

Tom DeWeese, "Agenda 21:
Conspiracy Theory or Threat,"
American Policy Center, May 12, 2012.

social justice. Social justice is an unnatural leveling of all wealth (other than that of the global elites); no one person is supposed to profit more than another.

Second E—Economic Prosperity

From *Wikipedia* comes this discussion of economic prosperity promoted under sustainable development:

> Economic growth is often seen as essential for economic prosperity, and indeed is one of the factors that is used as a measure of prosperity. The Rocky Mountain Institute has put forth an alternative point of view, that prosperity does not require growth, claiming instead that many of the problems facing communities are actually a result of growth, and that sustainable development requires abandoning the idea that growth is required for prosperity. The debate over whether economic growth is necessary for, or at odds with, human prosperity, has been active at least since the publication of "Our Common Future" in 1987, and has been pointed to as reflecting two opposing worldviews.

Keep in mind that almost every concept under Agenda 21 is written in newspeak—words often have the opposite meanings of those in your Webster dictionary so that the general public might be deceived, at least for a time (and it has been). Economic prosperity under Agenda 21 is anything but prosperity—other than for the global elites who are controlling the system. It is economic ruin for the ordinary people of the entire globe.

Agenda 21 proponents would have you believe that all of the wealth in the world was made on the backs of the poor and that the only way that this inequity can be corrected is to redistribute that wealth. While they claim that the wealth must be taken from the American middle class and given to the poor of the world, in actuality the money will be taken from that American middle class and given to the global elite (as if they didn't control most of the world's wealth already—

but that is not the issue; it is to reduce us to slaves at best). The poor, in Africa and other parts of the world, will never see a dime of the redistributed wealth; they are only the pretense for taking our money.

Agenda 21 encompasses the so-called free trade movement that created both NAFTA [North American Free Trade Agreement] and public-private partnerships which were incorporated into a government-driven economy called "corporatism." These public-private partnerships are nothing more than government-sanctioned monopolies—[Benito] Mussolini–style economics.

Third E—Ecological Integrity

To understand the power of the transformation of society under sustainable development, consider this quote from the UN's biodiversity treaty (which also was introduced at the Rio Earth Summit):

> "Nature has an integral set of different values (cultural, spiritual and material) where humans are one strand in nature's web and all living creatures are considered equal. Therefore the natural way is the right way and human activities should be molded along nature's rhythms."

This quote says it all; that we humans are nothing special—just one strand in the nature of things or, put another way, humans are simply biological resources. No better than slugs or dung. In fact, in the eyes of the globalists, we are of less value than slugs or dung. Their policy is to oversee any issue in which man interacts with nature—which, of course, is literally everything. This is necessary, they say, because humans only defile nature.

And private property ownership and control, along with individual and national sovereignty, are main targets of sustainable development. Consider this quote from the report of the UN's Habitat I conference:

"Land ... cannot be treated as an ordinary asset, controlled by individuals and subject to the pressures and inefficiencies of the market. Private land ownership is also a principle instrument of accumulation, and concentration of wealth, therefore, contributes to social injustice."

This mixture of socialism, fascism and corporatism (as Tom DeWeese so aptly pegs it), called Agenda 21, is the ruling force in our government today from the federal to the local. Not one of those ingredients would be allowed by our forefathers and not one is in sync with the Constitution; so how have we allowed all three to be combined into a recipe for global government and served to our unwitting nation?

| "After 2015 we should move from re-
ducing to ending extreme poverty, in
all its forms."

Poverty Must Be Eradicated to Achieve Global Sustainability

United Nations

*In July 2012, the secretary-general of the United Nations ap-
pointed Susilo Bambang Yudhoyono, Ellen Johnson Sirleaf, and
David Cameron as cochairpersons of a panel on the post-2015
development agenda. In the following viewpoint, the panel sum-
marizes its recommendations to the United Nations for the eradication of poverty through sustainable development. The panel
calls for five significant, transformational shifts: leave no one behind; put sustainable development at the core; transform economies for jobs and inclusive growth; build peace and effective,
open, and accountable institutions for all; and forge a new global
partnership.*

As you read, consider the following questions:

1. What are some examples of the reduction in poverty
   from 2000 to 2013 that the authors cite?

United Nations, "A New Global Partnership: Eradicate Poverty and Transform Economies Through Sustainable Development," New York: United Nations Publications, 2013.
Copyright © 2013 United Nations. Reprinted with the permission of the United Nations.

2. What were some of the elements lacking in the Millennium Development Goals, according to the viewpoint?

3. What are some of the massive changes in the world since 2000 and the changes likely to occur by 2030, according to the authors?

The panel [the High-Level Panel of Eminent Persons on the Post-2015 Development Agenda] came together with a sense of optimism and a deep respect for the Millennium Development Goals (MDGs). The 13 years since the millennium have seen the fastest reduction in poverty in human history: There are half a billion fewer people living below an international poverty line of $1.25 a day. Child death rates have fallen by more than 30%, with about three million children's lives saved each year compared to 2000. Deaths from malaria have fallen by one-quarter. This unprecedented progress has been driven by a combination of economic growth, better policies, and the global commitment to the MDGs, which set out an inspirational rallying cry for the whole world.

Building on Millennium Development Goals

Given this remarkable success, it would be a mistake to simply tear up the MDGs and start from scratch. As world leaders agreed at Rio in 2012, new goals and targets need to be grounded in respect for universal human rights, and finish the job that the MDGs started. Central to this is *eradicating extreme poverty* from the face of the earth by 2030. This is something that leaders have promised time and again throughout history. Today, it can actually be done.

So a new development agenda should carry forward the spirit of the Millennium Declaration and the best of the MDGs, with a practical focus on things like poverty, hunger, water, sanitation, education and health care. But to fulfil our vision of promoting sustainable development, we must go beyond the MDGs. They did not focus enough on reaching the very poorest and most excluded people. They were silent on the devastating effects of conflict and violence on development. The importance to development of good governance and institutions that guarantee the rule of law, free speech and open and accountable government was not included, nor the need for inclusive growth to provide jobs. Most seriously, the MDGs fell short by not integrating the economic, social, and environmental aspects of sustainable development as envisaged in the Millennium Declaration, and by not addressing the need to promote sustainable patterns of consumption and production. The result was that environment and development were never properly brought together. People were working hard—but often separately—on interlinked problems.

So the panel asked some simple questions: starting with the current MDGs, what to keep, what to amend, and what to add. In trying to answer these questions, we listened to the views of women and men, young people, parliamentarians, civil society organisations, indigenous people and local communities, migrants, experts, business, trade unions and governments. Most important, we listened directly to the voices of hundreds of thousands of people from all over the world, in face-to-face meetings as well as through surveys, community interviews, and polling over mobile phones and the Internet.

Massive Changes Since 2000

We considered the massive changes in the world since the year 2000 and the changes that are likely to unfold by 2030. There are a billion more people today, with world population at seven billion, and another billion expected by 2030. More than half of us now live in cities. Private investment in developing countries now dwarfs aid flows. The number of mobile phone subscriptions has risen from fewer than one billion to more than six billion. Thanks to the Internet, seeking business or information on the other side of the world is now routine for many. Yet inequality remains and opportunity is not open to all. The 1.2 billion poorest people account for only 1 per cent of world consumption while the billion richest consume 72 per cent.

Above all, there is one trend—climate change—which will determine whether or not we can deliver on our ambitions. Scientific evidence of the direct threat from climate change has mounted. The stresses of unsustainable production and consumption patterns have become clear, in areas like deforestation, water scarcity, food waste, and high carbon emissions. Losses from natural disasters—including drought, floods, and storms—have increased at an alarming rate. People living in poverty will suffer first and worst from climate change. The cost of taking action now will be much less than the cost of dealing with the consequences later.

Thinking about and debating these trends and issues together, the panelists have been on a journey.

At our first meeting in New York, the secretary-general charged us with producing a bold yet practical vision for development beyond 2015.

In London, we discussed household poverty: the daily reality of life on the margins of survival. We considered the many dimensions of poverty, including health, education and livelihoods, as well as the demands for more justice, better accountability, and an end to violence against women. We also heard inspiring stories of how individuals and communities have worked their way to prosperity.

In Monrovia, we talked about economic transformation and the building blocks needed for growth that delivers social inclusion and respects the environment: how to harness the ingenuity and dynamism of business for sustainable development. And we saw with our own eyes the extraordinary progress that can be made when a country once ravaged by conflict is able to build peace and security.

In Bali, we agreed on the central importance of a new spirit to guide a global partnership for a people-centred and planet-sensitive agenda, based on the principle of our common humanity. We agreed to push developed countries to fulfil their side of the bargain—by honouring their aid commitments, but also reforming their trade, tax and transparency policies, by paying more attention to better regulating global financial and commodity markets and by leading the way toward sustainable development. We agreed that developing countries have done much to finance their own development, and will be able to do more as incomes rise. We also agreed on the need to manage the world's consumption and production patterns in more sustainable and equitable ways. Above all, we agreed that a new vision must be universal: offering hope—but also responsibilities—to everyone in the world.

These meetings and consultations left us energized, inspired and convinced of the need for a new paradigm. In our view, business as usual is not an option. We concluded that the post-2015 agenda is a *universal agenda*. It needs to be driven by *five big, transformative shifts*:

Leave No One Behind

We must keep faith with the original promise of the MDGs, and now finish the job. After 2015 we should move from reducing to *ending* extreme poverty, in all its forms. We should ensure that no person—regardless of ethnicity, gender, geography, disability, race or other status—is denied universal human rights and basic economic opportunities. We should design goals that focus on reaching excluded groups, for example by making sure we track progress at all levels of income, and by providing social protection to help people build resilience to life's uncertainties. We can be the first generation in human history to end hunger and ensure that every person achieves a basic standard of well-being. There can be no excuses. This is a universal agenda, for which everyone must accept their proper share of responsibility.

Put Sustainable Development at the Core

For twenty years, the international community has aspired to integrate the social, economic, and environmental dimensions of sustainability, but no country has yet achieved this. We must act *now* to halt the alarming pace of climate change and environmental degradation, which pose unprecedented threats to humanity. We must bring about more social inclusion. This is a universal challenge, for every country and every person on Earth. This will require structural change, with new solutions, and will offer new opportunities. Developed countries have a special role to play, fostering new technologies and making the fastest progress in reducing unsustainable consumption. Many of the world's largest companies are already leading this transformation to a green economy in the context of sustainable development and poverty eradication. Only by mobilizing social, economic and environmental action together can we eradicate poverty irreversibly and meet the aspirations of eight billion people in 2030.

Transform Economies for Jobs and Inclusive Growth

We call for a quantum leap forward in economic opportunities and a profound economic transformation to end extreme poverty and improve livelihoods. This means a rapid shift to sustainable patterns of consumption and production-harnessing innovation, technology, and the potential of private business to create more value and drive sustainable and inclusive growth. Diversified economies, with equal opportunities for all, can unleash the dynamism that creates jobs and livelihoods, especially for young people and women. This is a challenge for every country on Earth; to ensure good job possibilities while moving to the sustainable patterns of work and life that will be necessary in a world of limited natural resources. We should ensure that everyone has what they need to grow and prosper, including access to quality education and skills, health care, clean water, electricity, telecommunications and transport. We should make it easier for people to invest, start up a business and to trade. And we can do more to take advantage of rapid urbanisation: Cities are the world's engines for business and innovation. With good management they can provide jobs, hope and growth, while building sustainability.

Build Peace and Effective, Open and Accountable Institutions for All

Freedom from fear, conflict and violence is the most fundamental human right, and the essential foundation for building peaceful and prosperous societies. At the same time, people the world over expect their governments to be honest, accountable and responsive to their needs. We are calling for a fundamental shift—to recognize peace and good governance as core elements of well-being, not optional extras. This is a universal agenda, for all countries. Responsive and legitimate institutions should encourage the rule of law, property rights, freedom of speech and the media, open political choice, access to justice, and accountable government and public institutions. We need a transparency revolution, so citizens can see exactly where and how taxes, aid and revenues from extractive industries are spent. These are ends as well as means.

Forge a New Global Partnership

Perhaps the most important transformative shift is toward a new spirit of solidarity, cooperation and mutual accountability that must underpin the post-2015 agenda. A new partnership should be based on a common understanding of our shared humanity, underpinning mutual respect and mutual benefit in a shrinking world. This partnership should involve governments but also include others: people living in poverty, those

with disabilities, women, civil society and indigenous and local communities, traditionally marginalised groups, multilateral institutions, local and national government, the business
community, academia and private philanthropy. Each priority
area identified in the post-2015 agenda should be supported
by dynamic partnerships. It is time for the international community to use new ways of working, to go beyond an aid
agenda and put its own house in order: to implement a swift
reduction in corruption, illicit financial flows, money launder-
ing, tax evasion, and hidden ownership of assets. We must
fight climate change; champion free and fair trade, technology
innovation, transfer and diffusion; and promote financial stability. And since this partnership is built on principles of
common humanity and mutual respect, it must also have a
new spirit and be completely transparent. Everyone involved
must be fully accountable.

From Vision to Action

We believe that these five changes are the right, smart and necessary thing to do. But their impact will depend on how they are translated into specific priorities and actions. . . .

The suggested targets are bold, yet practical. Like the MDGs, they would not be binding, but should be monitored closely. The indicators that track them should be disaggregated to ensure no one is left behind and targets should only be considered 'achieved' if they are met for all relevant income and social groups. We recommend that any new goals should be accompanied by an independent and rigorous monitoring system, with regular opportunities to report on progress and shortcomings at a high political level. We also call for a *data revolution* for sustainable development, with a new international initiative to improve the quality of statistics and information available to citizens. We should actively take advantage of new technology, crowd sourcing and improved connectivity to empower people with information on the progress toward the targets.

Taken together, the panel believes that these five fundamental shifts can remove the barriers that hold people back, and end the inequality of opportunity that blights the lives of so many people on our planet. They can, at long last, bring together social, economic and environmental issues in a coherent, effective and sustainable way. Above all, we hope they can inspire a new generation to believe that a better world is within its reach, and act accordingly.

> *"The U.S. should promote policies that actually contribute to development by allowing individuals to pursue their best interests, which collectively accelerate economic growth, development, and welfare."*

A Focus on Poverty Is the Wrong Way to Achieve Sustainable Global Growth

Brett D. Schaefer and Ambassador Terry Miller

Brett D. Schaefer is Jay Kingham Senior Research Fellow in International Regulatory Affairs at the Heritage Foundation. Ambassador Terry Miller is director of the Center for Trade and Economics at the Heritage Foundation. In the following viewpoint, Schaefer and Miller argue that the proposed United Nations (UN) Sustainable Development Goals (SDGs) are flawed and should not be endorsed by the United States. Some of the goals are imprecise or vague, and a number of them are driven by political agendas, they claim. Overall, the goals focus on the

Brett D. Schaefer and Ambassador Terry Miller, "U.N. Repeating Past Mistakes in New Sustainable Development Goals," Heritage Foundation, Issue Brief 4251, July 23, 2014. Copyright © 2014 by the Heritage Foundation. All rights reserved. Reproduced with permission.

symptoms of poverty and not the causes, Schaefer and Miller maintain. A better set of goals would focus on economic freedom and good governance, they conclude.

As you read, consider the following questions:

1. In which Millennium Development Goals has there been progress, according to the authors?

2. What evidence do the authors cite to support their claim that the United Nations is taking credit for progress it had no role in creating?

3. What are the three measures that the authors recommend the United States take to accelerate economic growth, development, and welfare?

The United Nations [U.N.] General Assembly is poised to adopt a new set of development criteria called the Sustainable Development Goals (SDGs) this September [2014]. The SDGs are intended to replace the Millennium Development Goals (MDGs) that expire at the end of 2015. Like the MDGs, the SDGs will involve a number of objectives that will be used by the U.N. to guide and measure progress on its global development agenda.

Such metrics can be a useful tool to measure progress, but the U.N. has allowed political priorities and slogans to distort the SDGs in a manner that undermines their utility, articulates goals in imprecise language that makes them unmeasurable or subjective, and implicitly endorses a top-down, input-driven development strategy that has not been successful historically. The U.S. should reject the SDGs as flawed and urge the U.N. to focus on encouraging countries to adopt policies known to facilitate economic growth and development: economic freedom and the rule of law.

The Modest Impact of the MDGs

The U.N. Millennium Declaration, adopted at the Millennium Summit in 2000, called for meeting specific development objectives by 2015—a process that resulted in eight MDGs to measure progress toward that pledge.

U.N. secretary-general Ban Ki-moon claims that the MDGs "have been the most successful global anti-poverty push in history." There has been progress toward a number of MDGs, including reducing the number of people in extreme poverty, access to potable water, and lower debt service ratios for developing nations. However, the U.N. is confusing cause and effect when it claims credit for this progress.

On reducing extreme poverty, for instance, the *Economist* observes, "China (which has never shown any interest in MDGs) is responsible for three-quarters of the achievement. Its economy has been growing so fast that, even though inequality is rising fast, extreme poverty is disappearing. China pulled 680m people out of misery in 1981–2010, and reduced its extreme-poverty rate from 84% in 1980 to 10% now." Indeed, much of the progress toward individual MDGs can be attributed to expanded economic growth, private investment, trade, and the policy changes that have facilitated this improvement. Development indicators such as the MDGs or the proposed SDGs can help assess the impact of these changes, but they do not cause them.

What the MDGs were successful at is focusing attention on increased funding for foreign assistance. Indeed, official development assistance has increased from $81.9 billion in 2000 to $134.7 billion in 2013. However, numerous studies find little evidence that increased official development assistance (ODA) leads to improved economic growth or development, and government development assistance is growing less relevant as private financial flows have grown in recent decades. According to the 2013 "Index of Global Philanthropy and Remittances," "Of the total financial flows from developed to developing countries, over 80% are private. Government aid, at less than 20%, is now a minority shareholder, the opposite of 40 years ago."

Moreover, an independent academic study assessing best and worst practices among aid agencies ranked U.N. agencies among the worst and least effective performers.

Flawed SDGs

The proposed list of objectives for the SDGs is a grab bag of 17 overarching goals, with over 100 subgoals, designed to satisfy multiple constituencies in the U.N. General Assembly and in the nongovernmental organization (NGO) community. In some instances, the objectives make sense in that they directly measure desired outcomes of development, such as alleviating poverty and hunger or improving health, education, and equality. Some goals are indirectly related, such as energy access, employment, industrialization, and strengthening the global partnership for sustainable development. Some are unrelated—such as halving the number of deaths from road traffic accidents globally—or even counterproductive, such as calls to reduce food price volatility through regulation of food commodity markets.

One example is a goal calling on developed countries to "implement fully ODA commitments to provide 0.7 percent of GNI [gross national income] in ODA to developing countries." This goal is economically flawed and makes no sense for development purposes. As stated in a 2005 study by the Center for Global Development:

> Originally intended as a political tool to goad rich countries to modestly increase their aid budgets, the specific figure of 0.7% was a compromise between educated guesses based on economic conditions in the early 1960s and on a crude and deeply flawed model of growth. . . . We find that if we apply the same assumptions that went into the original formulation to conditions present today, that the updated target

would be 0.01% of rich country income—well below current aid levels for all major donors.

Examples of imprecise or vague goals are replete, such as ensuring "significant mobilization of resources from a variety of sources to provide adequate and predictable means to implement programmes and policies to end poverty in all its dimensions" or to "substantially reduce the number of deaths and illnesses from air (indoor and outdoor), water and soil pollution." Targets such as these are impossible to measure and express little more than aspirations.

The opposite problem of overextension is just as prevalent. For instance, under the SDGs it is not enough to improve conditions; the SDGs aim grandly to "end poverty everywhere," "end hunger," "end child labor in all its forms," "eliminate gender disparities," "eliminate all forms of violence against all women and girls in public and private spaces," and "eliminate slums." These are positive aspirations to pursue, but they are not realistic goals to achieve.

Political agendas masquerading as development goals abound. The introduction contains lengthy reaffirmations of commitments to implement various environmental agreements, such as the Rio Declaration on Environment and Development, Agenda 21, and the Plan of Implementation of the World Summit on Sustainable Development. Goal 3.a is a call to "strengthen implementation of the [World Health Organization] Framework Convention on Tobacco Control." Goal 5.6 calls for ensuring "universal access to sexual and reproductive health and reproductive rights," which is a common euphemism in U.N. discussions for abortion.

The result is a dubious, impractical mix of commitments recycled from the MDGs, vaguely stated objectives that defy precise measurement, and politically popular agendas dressed up as development metrics.

A Better Way

The goal of reducing poverty is admirable and should be supported by the U.S. However, instead of focusing on U.N. metrics that are already tracked by international development agencies, the U.S. should promote policies that actually contribute to development by allowing individuals to pursue their best interests, which collectively accelerate economic growth, development, and welfare. Specifically, the U.S. should:

- Refuse to endorse the SDGs if they remain substantially similar to their current form. Although some SDGs are unobjectionable and could be useful, on balance they are simply a collection of political agendas and niche NGO causes.

- Seek to narrow the SDGs on core development goals and focus them on their only real purpose: to measure progress. The SDGs should be focused on metrics, not political agendas.

- Lead an effort to promote economic freedom and the rule of law. Numerous studies indicate that policy changes that create a more conducive environment for economic transactions, bolster a free and fair legal system, and strengthen government accountability and responsiveness are far more important to development than the amount of aid a country receives.

The Importance of Good Policy

While many individual SDG targets are desirable, the SDGs as a whole focus on the symptoms of poverty rather than the causes. If the U.S. is to help poor countries to develop, it should emphasize the importance of good policy in development, especially economic freedom, good governance, and the rule of law.

> *"Fundamentally, women everywhere want and acutely need sexual and reproductive health services to lead healthy sexual lives, have the number of children they want when they want them, deliver their babies safely and ensure that their newborns thrive."*

Gender Equality Is Key to Global Sustainability

Sneha Barot

Sneha Barot is a senior public policy associate at the Guttmacher Institute. In the following viewpoint, Barot says that as the United Nations negotiated and shaped a new development agenda in September 2015, delegates correctly included sexual and reproductive rights as essential to achieving gender equality. Research by the Guttmacher Institute in cooperation with the United Nations Population Fund documents substantial social and economic returns from meeting women's sexual and reproductive needs, she reports. Fully meeting these needs would save lives, reduce unwanted pregnancies, and reduce health care costs, Barot claims.

As you read, consider the following questions:

1. What are some of the negative health consequences of unintended pregnancy, according to the author?

2. How many women of reproductive age are there in the developing world, and how many of them are at risk of sexually transmitted infections, according to the author?

3. What would be the results if all 225 million women with an unmet need for modern contraception were able to receive it, according to the author?

Over the last three years, the international community of civil society advocates, policy makers, donors and multilateral agencies has devoted enormous resources to negotiate and shape a new global development agenda for adoption at the United Nations (UN) General Assembly in September 2015. This post-2015 development framework will build on the Millennium Development Goals, the current UN road map for tackling the world's problems related to poverty, development and sustainability set to expire later this year [2015]. In particular, the post-2015 framework will set forth a series of goals and targets on a range of issues critical to global development and environmental sustainability, likely including health, education, gender equality, protection and management of environmental resources, poverty, hunger and others. As such, its impact will be felt on development funding and programming for the next 15 years through its influence on national and donor priorities for the allocation of resources.

Delegates participating in the intergovernmental negotiations thus far have identified universal access to sexual and reproductive health care services and the fulfillment of reproductive rights as interventions integral to overall development goals related to ensuring healthy lives and achieving gender equality. This political support for sexual and reproductive health and rights is both sensible and strategic, given that the evidence shows that these investments are among the most effective in development.

Indeed, a new global analysis from the Guttmacher Institute, released jointly with the United Nations Population Fund (UNFPA), documents the substantial benefits that accrue from investing in a constellation of sexual and reproductive health services in several key areas: contraceptive services; pregnancy, delivery and newborn care; services and medicines for pregnant women living with HIV; and treatment for four other common STIs [sexually transmitted infections]. The research updates and quantifies the immediate and direct impact of these investments in terms of lives protected and dollars saved, as well as the synergies that can result from fully meeting a range of needs simultaneously. At the same time, there is a host of additional—but no less important—social and economic benefits for women, families and communities that flow from such investments.

Falling Far Short of the Need

In the last decade, the developing world as a whole has witnessed declines in maternal and infant deaths and rates of new HIV infection, which reflects increased international efforts in these health areas. Yet, progress has been uneven, and widespread disparities endure among and within countries. Guttmacher's new report, "Adding It Up: The Costs and Benefits of Investing in Sexual and Reproductive Health in 2014," finds that throughout the developing world, fulfillment of women's sexual and reproductive health needs is lacking. The report builds on previous analyses and calculates the costs and benefits of meeting the developing world's needs for contraceptive, maternal and newborn care. Moreover, for the first time, this analysis also includes services for pregnant women living with HIV and their newborns, and treatment for women with common STIs.

Contraception

"Adding It Up" documents that more than half of all women of reproductive age in developing regions are at risk of pregnancy and want to avoid a pregnancy in the next two years or longer. Yet, one-fourth of these women—225 million in 2014—are not practicing contraception or are using traditional methods such as withdrawal or common methods of periodic abstinence. These women have an unmet need for modern contraception. Accordingly, they are at high risk for a number of negative health consequences due to unintended pregnancy. Every year, 74 million unintended pregnancies occur in developing countries, which lead to an estimated 28 million unplanned births and 36 million abortions (20 million of which are unsafe). The vast majority of these unintended pregnancies—81%—occur among women with an unmet need for contraception. The reasons for this unmet need are many and varied.

Although more women are using modern contraceptives now than a decade ago, unmet need remains high worldwide. In fact, it has increased slightly since 2008, largely because levels of contraceptive use have not quite kept up with global population growth and the growing desire for smaller families. The problem of unmet need for modern contraception is not only persistent, but is concentrated among women wanting to avoid pregnancy who live in the poorest households, those with low education, teenage women and those living in rural areas. Within developing regions, this disparity plays out between poorer and wealthier areas. For example, sub-Saharan Africa and South Asia together account for 40% of women wanting to avoid pregnancy, but for 61% of women with unmet need for modern contraception.

Maternal and Newborn Health

Because the health of a mother and her newborn are closely intertwined, their care must also be linked. The World Health

Organization (WHO) has established standards to define a minimum level of care for all reproductive-age women and their infants—before and during pregnancy, during childbirth and after birth—to promote safe and healthy outcomes.

"Adding It Up" documents that among the 125 million women who give birth annually in developing regions, more than four in 10 do not obtain the minimum of four antenatal visits recommended by WHO. Even when they do make those visits, they do not receive all of the services that they need. About one-third of women across developing countries do not deliver their babies in a health facility, and this problem is particularly common in eastern Africa. Among women who experience an obstetric complication during pregnancy or delivery, such as hypertension, hemorrhage or obstructed labor, more than two-thirds do not receive the care that they need—either because they do not deliver in a health facility or that facility does not provide the necessary care. Moreover, more than two-thirds of newborns who need medical care for major complications do not receive it.

Women whose pregnancies do not result in a live birth—because of miscarriage, stillbirth or abortion—also need care, but a substantial portion does not receive it. For example, five million women in developing countries do not get facility-based care for a miscarriage or stillbirth, and just over three million women with complications from unsafe abortion do not receive post-abortion care.

Failing to meet women's contraceptive and maternal health care needs leads to an estimated 290,000 pregnancy-related deaths each year among women in developing countries, including 22,000 from unsafe abortions. In addition, 2.9 million babies die in the first month of life. Nearly all of these deaths among women and infants could be prevented with adequate medical care.

HIV and Other STIs

Of the 1.6 billion women of reproductive age in the developing world, an estimated 66 million are at high risk of STIs, including HIV, and need prevention information, education and services. Nearly 14 million women of reproductive age are living with HIV, including 11.6 million in sub-Saharan Africa. The global expansion of access to antiretroviral therapy has changed the course of the AIDS epidemic. Still, although just over two-thirds of women living with HIV need antiretroviral therapy, a large proportion (48%) of women living with HIV do not receive it.

Pregnant women living with HIV have heightened sexual and reproductive health needs, including treatment for their own health as well as prevention of HIV transmission to their infants. Each year, 273,000 infants become infected with HIV during pregnancy and delivery or through breast-feeding. Of the 1.5 million women with HIV who give birth each year, more than one-third do not receive the antiretroviral therapy they need during pregnancy to prevent this transmission to newborns, and three-quarters do not receive ongoing antiretroviral care to protect their own health.

STIs other than HIV are extremely common, but often go untreated—ultimately taking an enormous toll on women's reproductive health. Each year, about 200 million women of reproductive age are infected with one of four STIs: chlamydia, gonorrhea, syphilis and trichomoniasis. However, of those women, 82% do not receive services, even though all four STIs are curable. This gap may be due to a variety of factors, including asymptomatic infections, inadequate staff training and supplies, stigma surrounding STIs, and limited availability of STI testing and treatment in developing regions. However, untreated STIs can lead to serious health consequences, including infertility and increased risk of HIV acquisition, pregnancy complications and stillbirth.

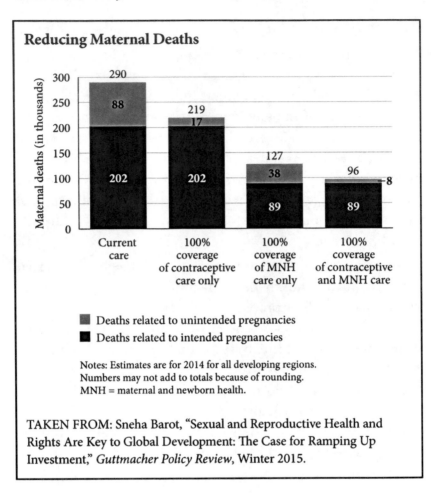

Reducing Maternal Deaths

Maternal deaths (in thousands)

- Current care: 290 (202 intended, 88 unintended)
- 100% coverage of contraceptive care only: 219 (202 intended, 17 unintended)
- 100% coverage of MNH care only: 127 (89 intended, 38 unintended)
- 100% coverage of contraceptive and MNH care: 96 (89 intended, 8 unintended)

▨ Deaths related to unintended pregnancies
■ Deaths related to intended pregnancies

Notes: Estimates are for 2014 for all developing regions.
Numbers may not add to totals because of rounding.
MNH = maternal and newborn health.

TAKEN FROM: Sneha Barot, "Sexual and Reproductive Health and Rights Are Key to Global Development: The Case for Ramping Up Investment," *Guttmacher Policy Review*, Winter 2015.

When Needs Are Met

Enabling women to plan their pregnancies and ensure healthy births would reap tremendous returns. If all 225 million women with an unmet need for modern contraception were to practice contraception, unintended pregnancies would drop by 70% and unsafe abortions would decline by 74%—leading to large and immediate health gains.

Fully meeting the unmet need for maternal and newborn health services would also lead to sizable declines in poor health outcomes. But because preventing unintended pregnancy is in itself a key component of improving maternal and newborn health outcomes, fully meeting the need for contraceptive care and maternal and newborn health care services simultaneously could achieve more dramatic improvements than investing in either one separately. In particular, fully meeting the need for these services, including HIV-related care for pregnant women and their newborns, would mean:

- maternal deaths would drop by two-thirds;

- newborn deaths would drop by three-fourths;

- the burden of disability related to pregnancy and delivery experienced by women and newborns would drop by three-fourths; and

- mother-to-newborn HIV transmission would be nearly eliminated.

"Adding It Up" does not estimate the impact of HIV prevention or treatment services more broadly. For other STIs, data are limited, but the report provides new evidence that fully meeting women's needs for chlamydia and gonorrhea treatment would prevent an additional 27 million women from developing pelvic inflammatory disease and seven million women from developing infertility.

Beyond all of these direct and striking health gains, there is a bounty of other social and economic returns yielded by meeting women's sexual and reproductive health needs. These benefits are felt from the micro to the macro level, by women, their families and their communities. When their needs are met, women and children are more likely to be able to stay in school and gain an education, which in turn will have a positive impact on their future labor force participation and earnings. Women experience an increase in social status, self-esteem and gender equity. Families face fewer orphaned children, and households can boost their savings and assets. Societies undergo improved living conditions, reduced poverty and fewer strains on environmental resources. All of these rippling benefits directly affect other global development goals.

Cost and Cost-Effectiveness

In 2014, the cost in developing countries for providing current levels of services related to modern contraception, maternal and newborn health care, HIV-related care for pregnant women and their newborns, and treatment for four common STIs totaled $18.6 billion. Fully meeting the need for this package of sexual and reproductive health services for women and their newborns would cost $39.2 billion annually, slightly more than double the current expenditure.

Although all of these investments yield tremendous benefits, some are so cost-effective that they offset the cost of other services. In particular, contraceptive services reduce unintended pregnancies and unplanned births which in turn lowers expenditures for maternal and newborn care, and frees up health system funds to provide other sexual and reproductive health services. In stark terms, every additional dollar invested in contraception reduces the cost of pregnancy-related care (including HIV care for pregnant women and newborns) by $1.47.

The case for combined investments makes sense in other ways, too. Sexually active women are exposed to multiple health risks from adolescence through their reproductive years. Opportunities for care are maximized when services are offered as interconnected parts of a continuum of care that supports women throughout their sexual and reproductive lives.

The bottom line is that investing in this integrated package of services is both effective and cost-effective. And at an annual cost of only $25 per woman of reproductive age in the developing world—or $7 per person—it is a "best buy" in development. Indeed, a group of leading economists associated with the think tank Copenhagen Consensus Center conducted a cost-benefit analysis in 2014 of the proposed targets and goals under the post-2015 development framework and rated investment in sexual and reproductive health as "phenomenal"—among the top 13 out of 169 targets.

Joining Evidence with Policy

Policy makers and other stakeholders involved in post-2015 negotiations should heed this overwhelming evidence that investing in sexual and reproductive health is effective and cost-effective, too. The post-2015 framework is important not only as a policy statement, but because it will guide funding priorities at the country and global levels. Indeed, achieving a global consensus that calls explicitly for robust support for sexual and reproductive health—and rights—increases the chances that women throughout the developing world will continue to see gains in their health and in their quality of life more broadly. Although access to sexual and reproductive health services is important, assuring sexual and reproductive rights is equally so, because women must possess the ability to make informed choices from among a range of high-quality methods and services freely and without discrimination. . . .

In this final year of post-2015 negotiations, government negotiators and civil society must grapple with many worthy competing priorities to formulate a consensus around a new global development framework. In addition, certain socially conservative countries and activists that are hostile to sexual and reproductive health and rights are sure to agitate specifically against addressing these issues in the final framework. The new evidence about the value and wisdom of investing in sexual and reproductive health and rights, however, is unequivocal. It reaffirms and bolsters the earlier research in this area and confirms that an individual's ability to attain sexual and reproductive health is essential and integral to societies' success in achieving sustainable development.

Fundamentally, women everywhere want and acutely need sexual and reproductive health services to lead healthy sexual lives, have the number of children they want when they want them, deliver their babies safely and ensure that their newborns thrive. And donors and developing nations alike have a responsibility to ramp up investment and support for sexual and reproductive health and rights, because all have a stake in the cascade of benefits that accrue to women, children, families, communities, countries and the planet.

> "If [the world survey's] recommendations were to be fully adopted by the UN's member states and carried out, it would mean the end of families as we know them."

Gender Equality Is an Assault on Life and Marriage

Steven W. Mosher

Steven W. Mosher is the president of the Population Research Institute and the author of Population Control: Real Costs, Illusory Benefits. *In the following viewpoint, Mosher argues that the United Nations (UN) world survey on the role of women in development uses terms like "equality" and "development" to promote its agenda of sterilization, abortion, and population control. When used by the UN, "reproductive health" is a code term for limiting population growth through contraception, abortion, and sterilization, he suggests. He contends that the form of gender equality advanced by UN feminists would threaten the institution of marriage worldwide.*

As you read, consider the following questions:

1. What is the goal of reproductive health programs, according to Mosher?

2. According to the viewpoint, what is the goal of radical environmentalists?

3. What do UN progressives mean by the term "gender," according to Mosher?

The new UN [United Nations] report on women makes for grim reading, if you can decipher it. The reason that you may have trouble doing so is that the report, called the "World Survey on the Role of Women in Development 2014: Gender Equality and Sustainable Development" is written in a kind of code. Words and expressions are used that sound reasonable—what could be wrong with "gender equality," for example?—but which, in the femspeak used by the UN, actually have quite radical and subversive meanings that are lost on the general public.

There is a reason for this linguistic deception. Properly understood, this world survey—the first published in five years—is nothing less than a battle plan for a deadly assault on life and marriage. If its recommendations were to be fully adopted by the UN's member states and carried out, it would mean the end of families as we know them, and a top-to-bottom restructuring of societies and economies as a whole.

If these revolutionary goals were clearly stated, the public outcry would be deafening, and resistance would grow. So UN bureaucrats disguise their true goals by using code words that only they and other progressives, who are also in the know, can understand.

Let me translate some of the world survey's recommendations back into plain, straightforward, unambiguous English, so you can better understand the road down which the UN wants to take us.

"Reproductive Health" = Sterilization Campaigns

The phrase "reproductive health," littered throughout the document, sounds unobjectionable. But it is actually a double deception, since it has nothing to do with reproduction and nothing to do with health. The goal of "reproductive health" programs is actually population control—reducing the birth rate by chemically or surgically disabling as many female reproductive systems as possible. For example, when the report says,

> "Respect, protect and promote sexual and reproductive health and rights for all, particularly women and girls, across the life cycle"

this should be read to mean that women and girls are encouraged to [use] contraception, sterilize, and abort their children. The reason why this "recommendation" is included in the section "On sustainable development," is that it is really about limiting population growth.

"Sustainable" = Limit, Restrict

Whenever you read the word sustainable, as in "Sustainable Development" or "Sustainable Population" you should substitute the words "limit" or "restrict." For example, when the report says,

> "Ground sustainable population policies in sexual and reproductive health and rights, including the provision of universally accessible quality sexual and reproductive health services . . ."

it actually means something like, "Population control policies should be based on the promotion of sterilization and abortion."

"Safe Abortion" = Abortion on Demand

Safe abortion sounds more woman-friendly than simply saying abortion. But it is used within the UN system to refer to the legalization of abortion on demand. So when you read,

> "Ground sustainable population policies in sexual and reproductive health and rights, including the provision of universally accessible . . . comprehensive sexuality education and safe abortion"

you should understand this to mean that "Population control policies should be based on cradle-to-grave sex education and the legalization of abortion on demand throughout all nine months of pregnancy."

"Gender Equality" = The End of Marriage

Under this seemingly harmless rubric—who could oppose equality between men and women?—hides a cultural revolution. For the kind of equality that UN bureaucrats have in mind would end the natural complementarity between the sexes that binds husband and wife together. Read the following sentence:

> "Recognize, reduce and redistribute unpaid care work between women and men within households, and between households and the state by expanding basic services and infrastructure that are accessible to all."

This really means that the radical feminists at the UN are instructing the nanny state to go into homes of their married citizens and force husbands and wives to do equal amounts of cooking, cleaning, child care, etc., regardless of their own preferences in the matter.

The notion of radical equality between men and women promoted by UN feminists also leads them to argue that, since men aren't burdened with childbirth, "equality" demands that women be permitted to have abortions to level the playing field, as it were.

"Sustainable development" is a catchphrase of the radical environmentalists who want to limit economic growth, which they see as harmful to the environment, by limiting population growth and resource use in poor countries. As the report advocates:

"Protect the commons and prevent the appropriation and exploitation of natural resources by private and public interests, through state oversight and multi-stakeholder regulation."

"Promote transitions to sustainable low-carbon, climate-resilient consumption and production patterns while ensuring gender equality."

These directives mean that land and mineral resources, regardless of the needs of the population, are to be set aside in nature preserves. Energy production and consumption are to be kept low.

And the population, it goes without saying, without access to resources and energy, will remain poor.

"Gender" =???

Most people think that the word "gender"—which appears in the UN report hundreds of times—is just another word for "sex." It isn't. As used by UN progressives, "gender" has nothing to do with fixed categories of male and female. It is not determined by one's anatomy and chromosomes. Instead, it is solely a matter of personal preference. One is "free" to be whatever "gender" one wants—or even, chameleon-like, to change from day to day.

There are currently 57 "gender" categories . . . and counting. (If you thought there are only six—male, female, LGBT [lesbian, gay, bisexual, and transgender]—you are behind the times.) Needless to say, this concept of "gender" is tremendously subversive, undermining marriages, families, and even society itself. (The lesbian mayor of Houston is a gender feminist, which is why, in that city, a biological male who is feeling feminine on a certain day can use the ladies' room.)

One-Child Policy = Forced Abortion

The UN report, which talks incessantly about protecting women's rights, hypocritically whitewashes China's brutal one-child policy. That hundreds of millions of women over the past 34 years have been aborted and sterilized, many under duress, goes unmentioned. Instead, we get the following bland paragraph:

> "The constitution of China mandates that the government support family planning and that individual couples practice it. The one-child policy, introduced in the late 1970s, has been implemented through a system of economic and social incentives and disincentives, along with free contraceptive services."

This should read: The Chinese Party–state [referring to the Communist Party of China] has taken control of the reproductive system of every women in the country, and violates their reproductive rights by controlling childbearing under a state plan, forcibly aborting and sterilizing them if they conceive a child without state permission.

But that would require the UN to acknowledge that abortion is a crime, and this the radical feminists at the UN would never do.

Periodical and Internet Sources Bibliography

The following articles have been selected to supplement the diverse views presented in this chapter.

Kiran Asher and Bimbika Sijapati Basnett — "Gender Equality and Sustainable Development as Human Rights: A Conversation," Center for International Forestry Research, February 4, 2015.

James A. Dorn — "Equality, Justice, and Freedom: A Constitutional Perspective," *Cato Journal*, Fall 2014.

Esther Duflo — "Women Empowerment and Economic Development," *Journal of Economic Literature*, vol. 50, no. 4, 2012.

Max Fisher — "The U.S. Is Catching Up to Europe on Gender Equality," *Washington Post*, October 25, 2012.

Phumzile Mlambo-Ngcuka — "Calling All Men: Gender Equality Isn't Just a Female Cause," *Time*, March 7, 2014.

Vivian Onano — "Young People at the Centre of Sustainable Development," *Huffington Post*, May 27, 2015.

Eduardo Porter — "Income Inequality Is Costing the U.S. on Social Issues," *New York Times*, April 28, 2015.

Eric A. Posner and Glen Weyl — "A Radical Solution to Global Income Inequality: Make the U.S. More Like Qatar," *New Republic*, November 6, 2014.

Erik Solheim — "To End Poverty We Also Need to Ensure Equality and Sustainability," *Guardian*, December 5, 2013.

Thomas Sowell — "Inequality Fallacies," *National Review Online*, January 21, 2014.

Jeff Turrentine — "Obama Will Abolish the Suburbs?," *Slate*, March 1, 2013.

OPPOSING VIEWPOINTS® SERIES

CHAPTER 4

Is Economic Growth Compatible with Sustainability?

Chapter Preface

In the six years since its inception, Uber, which is headquartered in San Francisco, has taken on the taxi industry and appears to be winning. Speaking at the DLD (Digital-Life-Design) conference in Munich in January 2015, Uber chief executive officer Travis Kalanick stated that while the taxi market in San Francisco is approximately $140 million per year, Uber is bringing in $500 million a year. As of June 2015, Uber's ride-sharing service was available in fifty-eight countries and three hundred cities, and *Forbes* called it the world's most highly capitalized start-up with a valuation of $50 billion. In contrast, rental car giant Hertz, a company that was started in 1918, has a market capitalization of $9.36 billion.

Uber is perhaps the most well known of businesses in the sharing economy, which is also known as collaborative consumption and the peer-to-peer marketplace. In the sharing economy, people share unused resources such as equipment, services, accommodations, or skills at a lower cost than the traditional retail or service provider. *Wikipedia*, which launched in January 2001, may have been the first entrant to the sharing economy. By 2011 the concept had caught on to the extent that *Time* magazine named collaborative consumption as one of the ten ideas that will change the world. Other companies in the sharing economy include Airbnb and Couchsurfing, apartment and house-sharing platforms; Lending Club and Prosper, peer-to-peer lending platforms; Kickstarter and Indiegogo, crowd-funding platforms; Lyft, Car2Go, and Zipcar, ride-sharing and car-sharing platforms; DogVacay, a dog boarding platform; and TaskRabbit, Zaarly, and LivePerson, knowledge and talent-sharing platforms. By 2025 PricewaterhouseCoopers estimates the five main sharing economy sectors that generated $15 billion in revenue in 2013 will generate $335 billion.

Proponents of the sharing economy say it provides both an attractive business model and a pathway to greater economic sustainability. Underused assets such as a spare bedroom, bike, or car can make money for their owners, and consumers save money because purchases in the sharing economy are typically cheaper than through a traditional service provider. Also heralded are the environmental benefits of the sharing economy, as renting a car rather than owning one means fewer cars are on the road. Researcher Juho Hamari and colleagues writing in the *Journal of the Association for Information Science and Technology* argue that collaborative consumption is both ecologically and economically sound, stating, "collaborative consumption has been expected to alleviate societal problems such as hyper-consumption, pollution, and poverty by lowering cost of economic coordination within communities."

However, the sustainability aspect of the sharing economy has come under attack by a number of commentators, who cite environmental issues as well as violations of workers' rights. According to Matthew Yeomans writing for *Inc.*, "On an environmental level, there are serious questions for all the transportation companies in this sector about whether their services are actually reducing the number of cars on the road—or just adding to the congestion by encouraging more people to drive for a living." Former US secretary of labor Robert Reich is sharply critical of the sharing economy for failing to address the social equity aspect of global sustainability:

> How would you like to live in an economy where robots do everything that can be predictably programmed in advance, and almost all profits go to the robots' owners? Meanwhile, human beings do the work that's *un*predictable—odd jobs, on-call projects, fetching and fixing, driving and delivering, tiny tasks needed at any and all hours—and patch together

barely enough to live on. . . . The euphemism is the "share" economy. A more accurate term would be the "share-the-scraps" economy.

The pros and cons of the sharing economy are among the topics debated in the following chapter, which examines whether economic growth is compatible with sustainability.

> *"At a time when we are rich in stuff and poor in leisure and joy, when we are stretching the limits of our health and the limits of the planet, economic growth is a labor of Sisyphus."*

We Can't Grow On

John de Graaf

John de Graaf is a member of the Earth Island Institute board of directors and coauthor of Affluenza: The All-Consuming Epidemic. *In the following viewpoint, de Graaf argues that economic growth is unsustainable. The current ways of propelling growth, such as fracking, are destructive to the environment, he claims. Growth does not bring happiness, as happiness levels since the 1950s are flat or in decline, despite the growth in per capita income, de Graaf suggests. A better alternative is to share jobs, work less, and spend more time on constructive and enjoyable activities, he concludes.*

As you read, consider the following questions:

1. What has been the result of the economic and population growth since World War II, according to the viewpoint?

2. What does Stefano Bartolini mean when he suggests that rapid economic growth is more a symptom of social decay than dynamism?

3. How does the author believe we can prevent unemployment as productivity increases?

It's a debate that's been with us at least since the dawn of the Industrial Revolution: Is economic growth sustainable, or at some point will we run up against resource scarcities? In its crudest form, the discussion comes down to disagreement between Malthusians, who say that at some point we'll overreach the planet's carrying capacity, and Cornucopians, who argue that human ingenuity and technological progress will overcome physical limits. The debate has taken on new urgency today as global climate change and an ever increasing human population put new strains on resources. John de Graaf, director of the film *Affluenza* and writer of an accompanying book, says the market economy's constant drive for growth is incompatible with a finite planet. Roger Pielke Jr., an environmental studies professor at the University of Colorado, disagrees, and says that to be anti-growth is to argue for keeping poor people poor.

Is economic growth sustainable? Is it desirable? First, let's define our terms. I'm speaking of material growth, more products for more people. Non-material "development"—including improvements in health, education, and leisure time—may well be sustainable and desirable. But further material growth, especially in rich countries, is much harder to justify.

The twentieth-century environmentalist David Brower pointed out that, since World War II, population and economic growth have resulted in greater material consumption than in all previous human history. In that period—one one-hundredth of a second if we compress the age of Earth into a single week—we have reduced our fisheries, fossil fuels, and soils by half while causing the extinction of countless species and dangerously changing the climate.

Consider what it means that we did this in the blink of the geological eye. There are those who believe what we've been doing for that last hundredth of a second can go on indefinitely. Those people are, Brower observed, considered reasonable and intelligent human beings. Indeed, they run our governments and industries. But they are stark raving mad. It may be hard to convince our leaders to turn away from growth, but not as hard as changing the laws of physics.

Simply put: We can't grow on like this.

The Global Footprint Network finds that we already use far more resources and produce more waste than is sustainable, if by "sustainable" we mean replicable for any meaningful amount of time. Were every country to suddenly adopt the US lifestyle, we'd need four more planets.

Technical improvements can reduce the impact of each additional unit of growth. But such "decoupling" is partial. Total resource use and throughput continue to rise via the so-called "Jevons paradox"—e.g., we get better gas mileage, but we then drive more, or use our savings to fly more, using more total energy. As the ecological economist Tim Jackson puts it: "Resource efficiency is going in the wrong direction. Even relative decoupling isn't happening."

Meanwhile, we seek new but more dangerous means to propel continued growth: fracking, tar sands mining, and costly, potentially catastrophic nuclear technologies. Even solar and wind technologies require increased strip-mining of copper, threatening wild areas like Bristol Bay. The potential consequences of environmental crises increase with more complex and vulnerable technologies. These technological "breakthroughs" are assumed to be evidence against limits to growth, when they are but temporary stopgaps.

Democrats and Republicans alike believe growth is essential and desirable. Yet the record is mixed, at best. Economic

Why Is Economic Growth a Threat to Economic Sustainability?

To grow, an economy requires more natural capital, including soil, water, minerals, timber, other raw materials, and energy sources. When the economy grows too fast or gets too big, this natural capital is depleted, or "liquidated." To function smoothly, the economy also requires an environment that can absorb and recycle pollutants. When natural capital stocks are depleted, and/or the capacity of the environment to absorb pollutants is exceeded, the economy is forced to shrink.

Brian Czech, "FAQs,"
Center for the Advancement of the Steady State Economy.

growth increases happiness when countries are poor, but these benefits level off as they grow beyond a modest level of comfort. The United States is the best example of this. Per capita income has tripled since the 1950s, but happiness levels have been flat or falling, according to yearly surveys conducted by Gallup.

Impoverished countries still need to grow; modest growth in the past five years, for example, increased happiness in Angola by 25 percent, according to the UN's 2013 "World Happiness Report." But they must grow carefully, not as new consumer societies permeated by market values. And greater growth in rich countries is not only unsustainable but counterproductive. In the United States, doctors call stress from overwork "the new tobacco" while depression and loneliness are soaring.

Italian economist Stefano Bartolini suggests that rapid economic growth is more a symptom of social decay than dynamism. The drive to grow leads to longer working hours and loss of natural habitat. Social connection is lost to overwork, but sold back to us as consumer products we presume will make us happy. We alleviate our loss of nature by flights to gorgeous tropical beaches. All these defensive expenditures result in greater growth, exacerbating resource depletion and climate change.

We are told we must grow to provide employment and "lift all boats." Yet the past 35 years of growth have done neither; growth has been siphoned into the pockets of the already wealthy, creating a Grand Canyon between rich and poor in the US as well as globally. Eighty-five billionaires now own as much wealth as the bottom half of the planet's population. Growth-driven economic policies have led to elimination of jobs through outsourcing and automation, trends that show no sign of abating. Faith in a bigger pie as the great equalizer only delays fair wealth redistribution.

Yet if we don't grow, how can we prevent unemployment as productivity increases? [Karl] Marx, [John Maynard] Keynes and other great economists were clear about this: We should share the jobs and work less. That is still the way forward. Trading productivity for leisure instead of stuff will allow us to reduce unemployment, while giving everyone time for social connection and recreation. Limits on working hours would give us time to restore neighborhoods, grow some of our own food, de-stress, and engage in our own favorite artistic, athletic, and cultural activities.

Fifty years ago, in his "Great Society" speech, Lyndon Johnson warned that the values and beauty of our nation were being "buried by unbridled growth." A Great Society, he said, would judge itself not by the quantity of its goods, but the quality of its goals. At a time when we are rich in stuff and poor in leisure and joy, when we are stretching the limits of our health and the limits of the planet, economic growth is a labor of Sisyphus.

Environmentalists should turn a deaf ear to the siren song of growth. The good life lies beyond, and we can have it if we choose.

> *"Free markets are the most robust
> mechanism ever devised by humanity
> for delivering rapid feedback on how
> decisions turn out."*

Free Market Economic Growth Is Sustainable

Ronald Bailey

Ronald Bailey is science correspondent for Reason *magazine. In the following viewpoint, Bailey maintains that free market capitalism is the only economic system that meets the criterion for sustainable development—development that meets the needs of the present without compromising the future. Civilizations advance because they are able to foresee problems and successfully address them, he posits. Free market societies excel at using the trial-and-error method to problem solve, Bailey states. The spread of democratic capitalism is the best way to improve the lot of people worldwide, he concludes.*

As you read, consider the following questions:

1. What are natural statutes, according to the author?

Ronald Bailey, "Free Markets=Sustainable Development: Without Capitalism, True Sustainability Is Impossible," *Reason*, June 12, 2012. Copyright ©2012 Reason.com. Copyright © 2012 by Reason.com. All rights reserved. Reproduced with permission.

2. What are open access orders, according to the author?

3. What is the only way to improve the lot of hundreds of millions of people worldwide, and why, according to the author?

"The current global development model is unsustainable." That is the conclusion of the High-Level Panel on Global Sustainability, appointed earlier this year [2012] by United Nations [U.N.] secretary-general Ban Ki-moon to outline the economic and social changes needed to achieve global sustainability. The panel urged the world leaders who will gather in Rio de Janeiro next week for the U.N. Conference on Sustainable Development to embrace "a new approach to the political economy of sustainable development."

Little Sustainability or Development Throughout History

The panel's report, "Resilient People, Resilient Planet: A Future Worth Choosing," specifically cited the definition of sustainable development devised in "Our Common Future," another U.N. report from an expert panel headed by former Norwegian prime minister Gro Harlem Brundtland issued in 1987. "Sustainable development is development that meets the needs of the present without compromising the ability of future generations to meet their own needs," declared the Brundtland report.

It turns out that the only form of society that has so far met this criterion is democratic free-market capitalism. How can that be? Let's take a look at the two terms, *sustainable* and *development*. With regard to most of human history there has been precious little in the way of "development." The vast majority of people lived and died in humanity's natural state of disease-ridden abject poverty and pervasive ignorance. Economic historian Angus Maddison calculated that per capita Western European incomes in 1 A.D. averaged $600 and rose by 1500 to $800 reaching $1,200 by 1820. In China average per capita income was $450 in 1 A.D. rising by 1500 to $600 and reaching $700 by 1820. And the rise was anything but steady, e.g., income in Western Europe fell from the early Roman Empire average to $425 by 1000 A.D.

And what about the other term, *sustainable*? Again, looking across history and the globe, we know for a fact that there have been, until now, no sustainable societies. All of the earlier civilizations in both the Old and New Worlds collapsed at various times, e.g., Babylonia, Rome, the Umayyad Caliphate, Harappa, Gupta, Tang, Maya, Olmec, Anasazi, Moche, just to mention a few. Of course, collapse in this context doesn't mean that everybody died, but that their ways of life radically shifted and often much of the population migrated to other regions. In other words, history provides us with no models of sustainable development other than democratic capitalism.

Every one of these earlier ultimately unsustainable societies were what economics Nobelist Douglass North and his colleagues call "natural states" in *Violence and Social Orders: A Conceptual Framework for Interpreting Recorded Human History*. Natural states are basically organized as hierarchical patron-client networks in which small militarily potent elites extract resources from a subject population. The basic deal is a Hobbesian [relating to the English philosopher Thomas Hobbes] contract in which elites promise their subjects an end to the "war of all against all" in exchange for wealth and power.

Natural states operate by limiting access to valuable resources, e.g., by creating and sharing the rewards of monopolies. One fundamental downside to this form of social organization is that innovation, both social and technological, is stifled because it threatens the monopolies through which elite patrons extract wealth. While natural states do succeed in dramatically reducing interpersonal violence, they have one appalling consequence as Maddison's data show: persistently low average incomes. Again, as history teaches, civilizations organized as natural states are not sustainable in the long run.

Three Theories of Unsustainability

Lots of thinkers have pondered what causes the collapse of civilizations, i.e., why they are unsustainable over the long run. Let's take a brief look at three recent theories of unsustainability: climate change, complexity, and self-organized criticality cascades. In the January 26, 2001, issue of *Science*, Yale University anthropologist Harvey Weiss and University of Massachusetts geoscientist Raymond Bradley asked, "What Drives Societal Collapse?" They concluded, "Many lines of evidence now point to climate forcing as the primary agent in repeated social collapse." Basically they argue that abrupt and long-lasting droughts caused the downfalls of civilizations in both the Old and New Worlds.

Utah State University anthropologist Joseph Tainter, author of the 1988 classic *The Collapse of Complex Societies*, asserts that societies fall apart when their problem-solving institutions fail. Tainter argues, "Confronted with problems, we often respond by developing more complex technologies, establishing new institutions, adding more specialists or bureaucratic levels to an institution, increasing organization or regulation, or gathering and processing more information."

Tainter maintains that this strategy of building complex institutions ultimately fails as the result of diminishing marginal returns to the social investment in them. Collapse occurs when accumulating unaddressed problems overwhelm a society. Interestingly, Tainter notes, "In a hierarchical institution, the flow of information from the bottom to the top is frequently inaccurate and ineffective."

In a 2002 article, "Why Do Societies Collapse?," published in the *Journal of Theoretical Politics*, independent political scientist Gregory Brunk argues that societies are self-organizing critical systems. The usual example of self-organizing criticality is a sand pile in which grains of sand are constantly being added. Many land and simply find a place in the pile; some grains land and cause small local avalanches that soon come to rest; and eventually a grain lands that causes a huge avalanche that changes the shape of the whole pile. In a 2009 article, "Society as a Self-Organized Critical System," in *Cybernetics and Human Knowing*, researchers Thomas Kron and Thomas Grund suggest the example of the start of World War I as a social avalanche. In that case, an unlikely series of events involving a lost driver gave Serbian nationalist assassin Gavrilo Princip the opportunity to kill Franz Ferdinand, the archduke of the Austrian-Hungarian Empire, and his wife, Sophie. And as the phrase goes, the rest was history.

Brunk suggests the main mechanism by which societies reach a critical point where collapses are realized was outlined by economist Mancur Olson in his 1982 book *The Rise and Decline of Nations: Economic Growth, Stagflation, and Social Rigidities*. Olson argued that over time interest group politics produces over-bureaucratization, essentially recreating the patron-client networks characteristic of natural states.

These three theories of societal collapse can complement one another. Long-duration intense local droughts would no doubt constitute a problem that complex hierarchical institutions would have difficulty solving, thus producing a criticality cascade that results in social collapse. It's important to stress that all of the social collapses cited by these authors occurred with natural states, that is, societies organized as patron-client networks. In fact, the more recent social collapses, e.g., the Soviet Union, Yugoslavia, the [Democratic Republic of the] Congo, Somalia, and Libya, all also occurred in residual natural states that had persisted into the modern era.

The plain fact is that development (rising incomes, health, and education) occurred only after what North and his colleagues identify as a new form of social organization, open access orders, arose during the past two centuries. Open access orders are basically societies organized as democratic free-market capitalism, and are characterized by the rule of law, the proliferation of private economic, social, religious, and political institutions, and civilian control of the military. In all of history, the only kind of development has been capitalist development, along with parasitical versions of development that some remaining natural states can attain for a while by imitating aspects of open access borders. By 2008, average per capita income in Western Europe was $22,200 and in China $6,800.

Free-Market Development

Is free-market development sustainable? After all, it's only been around for 200 years. Obviously, most of the folks gathering next week at the U.N. conference in Rio don't think so. Last September a U.N.-sponsored activist conference issued a declaration, "Sustainable Societies, Responsive Citizens," that urged the replacement of "the current economic model, which promotes unsustainable consumption and production patterns, facilitates a grossly inequitable trading system, fails to eradicate poverty, assists in the exploitation of natural resources to the verge of extinction and total depletion, and has induced multiple crises on Earth" with "sustainable economies in the community, local, national, regional and international spheres."

Perhaps free-market capitalism will prove itself unsustainable in the long run. But I don't think so. Brunk suggests that humans don't just take complexity cascades (avalanches) lying down; they attempt to foresee and dampen them. "From this perspective, *the fundamental reason that civilization has advanced is because societies have become more adept in addressing the problems caused by complexity cascades*" [emphasis in original], claims Brunk. The chief way in which modern societies have "become more adept in addressing the problems caused by complexity cascades" is free markets. Free markets

The World Must Shift to a Sustainable Economy

We are convinced that our planet and the human-earth community will only survive, thrive and prosper by shifting to an economy that is sustainable, equitable and focused on the elimination of the extremes of wealth and poverty through the actions of responsive citizens and volunteerism.

We note that unsustainable consumption and production patterns have been major contributors to climate change and poverty and that sustainable development can only be ensured if humanity, directed and led by government policies, embraces humane, sustainable, low-carbon lifestyles and adopts sustainable livelihoods.

We also note that sustainable lifestyles and livelihoods must be built on sustainable consumption and production in our globalizing world and equity among generations, genders, nations, cultures and languages.

We acknowledge that sustainable consumption, in particular, needs to consider the minimization of the environmental impact of purchasing decisions and the maximization of the social impact of our purchases.

We reaffirm consequently that individuals, families and communities are key actors in achieving sustainable consumption and production and should be empowered and enabled through education in everyday life competencies to assume responsibility for achieving sustainable lifestyles all around the world.

Peter Wittig,
"Letter Dated 7 October 2011 from the Permanent Representative of Germany to the United Nations Addressed to the President of the General Assembly," United Nations, March 20, 2012.

are the most robust mechanism ever devised by humanity for delivering rapid feedback on how decisions turn out. Profits and losses discipline people to learn quickly from and fix their mistakes. Consequently, markets are superb at using trial and error to find solutions to problems. What about the Brundtland report criterion? As I have argued elsewhere, "There is only one proven way to improve the lot of hundreds of millions of poor people, and that is democratic capitalism. It is in rich democratic capitalist countries that the air and water are becoming cleaner, forests are expanding, food is abundant, education is universal, and women's rights respected. Whatever slows down economic growth also slows down environmental improvement." By vastly increasing knowledge and pursuing technological progress, past generations met their needs and vastly increased the ability of our generation to meet our needs. We should do no less for future generations.

Top-down bureaucratization of the sort favored by the delegates who will be meeting in Rio moves societies back in the direction of natural states in which monopolies are secured and run by elites. Innovation would thus stall and the ability of people and societies to adapt rapidly to changing conditions, economic and ecological, via free markets and democratic politics, would falter. "Ironically, instead of eliminating all complexity cascades, what the increasing bureaucratization of mature societies may do is increase the impact of the really big cascades when they overwhelm a society's barricades," argues Brunk. That's entirely correct.

What well-meaning activists and U.N. bureaucrats are trying to do is centrally plan the world's ecology. History suggests that that would work out about as well for humanity and the natural world as centrally planned economies did.

> *"There is little doubt that through the time-honoured act of sharing we can strengthen communities, reduce consumption and facilitate the nonmonetary distribution of goods and services."*

A Sharing Economy Is Necessary for Global Sustainability

Rajesh Makwana

Rajesh Makwana is the executive director of Share The World's Resources. In the following viewpoint, Makwana argues that if the sharing economy is to create a more equitable economic system, its definition must be broadened beyond its current emphasis on individuals and businesses to encompass international and national governing bodies. Care must be taken to prevent the co-option of sharing for commercial gain by the corporate sector, he warns. True economic sharing has the power to create a world that is more equitable while protecting the environment, Makwana contends.

Rajesh Makwana, "Global Justice, Sustainability and the Sharing Economy," Share: The World's Resources, June 3, 2014. Copyright © 2014 by Share: The World's Resources. All rights reserved. Reproduced with permission.

As you read, consider the following questions:

1. How fast is humanity as a whole consuming natural resources, according to Makwana?

2. What is "sharewashing," and why is it problematic, according to the viewpoint?

3. What should be done to prevent sharing from being co-opted by venture capitalists and the corporate sector, according to Makwana?

With public interest in the sharing economy on the rise, a polarisation of views on its potential benefits and drawbacks is fast becoming apparent. Much of the mainstream media continues to focus on the ability of the sharing economy to generate wealth and create new billionaires, while some social entrepreneurs and progressives claim that interpersonal sharing is the solution to the world's most intractable problems. At the same time, a growing number of analysts are concerned that the sharing economy could enable businesses to evade regulations and even break the law. These increasingly conflicting views reflect the diverse interests of the many individuals, organisations and businesses engaged in what is essentially an emerging movement for sharing that has yet to clarify its purpose.

Differing Definitions of the Sharing Economy

To add a further layer of confusion to the debate, there is little agreement on what the sharing economy actually is. For example, Rachel Botsman—a leading proponent of the 'what's mine is yours' philosophy—argues that the sharing economy forms part of a much wider collaborative economy that leverages technology and trust to facilitate a more efficient distribution of goods and services. A broader definition has been put forward by The People Who Share, who regard the sharing economy as an "alternative socio-economic system which embeds sharing and collaboration at its heart—across all aspects of social and economic life". Friends of the Earth have also significantly expanded the discourse on sharing to include the political sphere, albeit focussing on city-wide sharing as a means for improving environmental sustainability and equity among citizens.

All of these existing definitions still pay insufficient attention to national and global forms of economic sharing, particularly those facilitated by democratically elected governments. Instead, the focus generally remains limited to individual (peer-to-peer) and local sharing initiatives. Apart from those advocating for localised forms of sharing to be replicated in cities across the world, rarely is the sharing economy discussed in terms of systems of sharing and redistribution that operate on a nationwide or global scale, or in relation to calls for governments to institute the more transformative forms of economic sharing that are possible today.

This is not to deny the very real potential of the sharing economy to help strengthen communities, reduce the rate at which resources are consumed, and create financial returns at very low marginal cost. However, if our reason for supporting different modes of sharing is a desire to create a more equitable and sustainable economic system, we need to significantly broaden our understanding and interpretation of what constitutes a sharing economy. There is no question that it makes sound economic and environmental sense for businesses and individuals to reduce their carbon footprints and share scarce resources. But government policy (enacted either nationally or through international agreements) ultimately determines how effectively nations and the international community can address the underlying causes of inequality, climate change and resource wars—some of the most pressing challenges that face humanity in the 21st century.

Bearing in mind the urgent need to implement sharing on a systemic and global basis, a fresh evaluation of the sharing economy from the perspective of social justice and environmental sustainability is presented below. The five general positions that follow do not present a comprehensive critique by any standards, but they are a starting point for broadening the sharing economy discourse and making it more relevant to the bigger-picture issues that concern many progressives today. In particular, this perspective questions the role of commerce in so-called sharing-related business activities. It also proposes that we should include long-standing national and global forms of sharing in our definition of what constitutes a sharing economy, especially if we are working toward the creation of a more equal, just and sustainable world.

More Is Needed than Interpersonal Forms of Sharing

There is good reason to doubt whether the sharing economy (at least as it is generally understood today in terms of peer-to-peer activities) can ever have a significant impact on pressing global crises. For example, many people involved in the sharing economy aim to reduce their personal consumption to sustainable levels. While this is an important practice, the sheer scale of the ecological crisis suggests that simply sharing surplus or under-utilised personal goods is not a sufficient response to a global problem that requires systemic change at all levels to resolve. As often repeated, humanity as a whole is consuming natural resources 50% faster than the planet can replenish them. Not only is this massive overshoot in global consumption levels set to worsen as the world's consumer class expands, it is also further complicated by huge imbalances. Around 20% of the world's population are responsible for 80% of all resource consumption, while the remaining 80% are surviving on a 'low consumption pathway' and 20% are in 'basic needs deficit.'

Clearly the global sustainability crisis cannot be addressed effectively until the structural factors that are responsible for creating these inequalities are fully addressed, and this has huge implications for transforming government policies and economic systems both nationally and globally. A huge array of reforms is needed to reconfigure the way nations extract, produce, distribute and consume resources across the world. For instance, this would include rethinking our notions of progress and prosperity, ending the dominance of consumption-led economic growth over government policy, and reversing the relentless push toward trade liberalisation. As endlessly debated by civil society groups, much also needs to be done to dismantle the culture of consumerism, reconceptualise financial measures like GDP [gross domestic product], and shift investment toward building and sustaining a low-carbon infrastructure. . . .

If advocates of the sharing economy are really motivated to tackle complex social and ecological issues, they should also devote time and energy to promoting forms of sharing that are far more effective at addressing these problems, such as universal social protection or contraction and convergence approaches to addressing climate change. This means moving beyond the solely personal, community and city-oriented view of sharing, and embracing a wider understanding of sharing that includes the role of governments in advancing effective social policy and environmental regulations. Most of all, it is at the national and global level that the sharing economy can be revolutionary and transformative—if its supporters are willing to engage in the gritty politics of reforming government policy to establish truly effective and 'sharing' societies.

A Broader Definition of Sharing Is Needed

Existing definitions of the sharing economy tend to focus on personal, local and business approaches to sharing, even when those involved in the sharing movement profess to care deeply about climate change and other global issues. But these definitions present a very limited and superficial understanding of what the sharing economy is, which disconnects the sharing economy movement from serious attempts to address social injustice or environmental degradation. For instance, national systems of sharing are arguably the most established, important and fundamental examples of sharing economies that exist in the modern world, as alluded to above. Through systems of progressive taxation and the provision of essential public services and social protection for all, the vast majority of people in most developed countries are involved in and benefit from these broad-based sharing systems. Why aren't these crucial examples of sharing part of the discourse and evolving definition of the sharing economy? . . .

Supporters of peer-to-peer sharing could help build a much stronger identity by recognising that their activities form part of these much broader and more fundamental sharing systems that operate at all levels of society. An inclusive working definition that can embrace the diverse national and international forms of sharing was put forward in STWR's [Share The World's Resources] report "Financing the Global Sharing Economy," and is worth revisiting:

"The sharing economy is a broad term used in this report that encompasses the many systems of sharing and redistribution that exist locally, nationally and globally—whether facilitated by individuals, states or other institutions. It is concerned with the social, economic, environmental, political and spiritual benefits of sharing both material and non-material resources—everything from time and love to money and natural resources."

"In comparison, the global sharing economy refers specifically to systems of sharing and redistribution that are international or global in nature—whether facilitated directly by people and governments or by global institutions like the United Nations. It refers to the many methods by which the international community can share their financial, technical, natural and other resources for the common good of all people. The global sharing economy is still in its infancy, but is nonetheless an important expression of the growing sense of solidarity and unity between people and nations."

Co-optation by the Corporate Sector Must Be Resisted

In a worrying phenomenon sometimes described as 'sharewashing', commercial activities that have never before been regarded as sharing are now rebranded under this trendy new meme. For example, most people would agree that renting is not the same as sharing and neither is giving people a lift in your car in exchange for cash. Room-sharing and car-sharing enterprises might offer excellent and rewarding services in their own right, but they may have little to do with the principle of sharing in relation to human rights and concerns for equity, democracy, justice and sustainability, especially when the main beneficiaries are company shareholders and not customers or employees. It is already well recognised that many so-called sharing enterprises adopt business models and ethics that do not allow wealth, income or decision making to be shared with their employees or customers to any significant extent.

Above all, we must guard against sharing-oriented initiatives from being co-opted by the corporate sector. Rampant commercialisation is at the heart of the social and environmental problems we face, so those involved in the sharing economy movement should be cautious about supporting large corporations whose wider business models and practices fail to embody the principle of sharing in any real sense. This sort of co-optation is a well-documented phenomenon in relation to social and environmental issues, with the 'greenwashing' of oil companies that supposedly pursue an ecological agenda, and the 'whitewashing' of unethical corporations through corporate social responsibility programs.

If sharing is not to be co-opted by venture capital and the corporate sector, perhaps there should be a minimum criteria for any company that professes to be part of the sharing economy. At the very least, sharing economy businesses should be set up as not-for-profits or cooperatives, or else they should adopt business models that promote the triple bottom line of people, planet and profit. They must also pay their fair share of taxes, as this is a key part of the established and most important system of sharing that we have (yet) created.

Sharing Is a Cause for the Global Justice Movement

Many supporters of sharing economy initiatives think that sharing is fashionable and trendy—a lifestyle choice—and that by sharing they are doing their bit to promote egalitarian or environmentally conscious ethics and values. But if the sharing movement is to play a role in shifting society away from the dominant economic paradigm and help to resolve global crises, it will have to get political. This means recognising that sharing economy advocates are part of a much larger body of people calling for more transformative forms of economic sharing in relation to pressing social and environmental concerns.

Millions of people across the world are already campaigning for economic and political reforms that embody the principle of sharing, although they don't always use the term 'sharing' in their advocacy and activities. The sharing of wealth, power or resources is central to what progressives have long been calling for, and supporting these demands for social justice, peace and ecological sustainability is fundamental to affecting structural change on the scale that is now necessary. This means being more aware of the issues that environmentalists and activists campaign on, and explicitly aligning local sharing activities with their broader justice-based vision of economic and ecological sharing. . . .

People Are at the Center of a Sharing Economy

People are at the heart of a sharing economy; it is a people's economy, meaning that people are active citizens and participants of their communities and the wider society. The participants of a sharing economy are individuals, communities, companies, organisations and associations, all of whom are deeply embedded in a highly efficient sharing system, to which all contribute and benefit from. Human rights are respected and safeguarded. People are also suppliers of goods and services; they are creators, collaborators, producers, coproducers, distributors and redistributors. In a sharing economy, people create, collaborate, produce and distribute peer to peer, person to person.

Benita Matofska,
"What Is the Sharing Economy?"
The People Who Share.

The Sharing Economy Appeals to Intrinsic Values

It is not hard to imagine how a process of sharing could theoretically play a key role in addressing multiple global crises, as genuine forms of economic sharing should result in a fairer distribution of resources for all people within planetary limits. However, there is a great deal of evidence to suggest that promoting the sharing economy as another way to supplement our income is likely to promote extrinsic values that will undermine efforts to create a more equitable and sustainable world. According to detailed studies, promoting intrinsic values that go beyond concerns about oneself are far more likely to encourage sustainable lifestyles than a focus on extrinsic values, such as personal financial gain. In other words, those who share because they are told it can help them make some spare cash are less likely to engage in other environmentally beneficial activities, compared to those who share out of purely environmental concerns.

Of course, there is nothing wrong with making some extra money or being motivated by extrinsic values. However, if our goal is to help address the world's interconnected and intractable crises, the evidence suggests that our campaigning activities must remain firmly aligned to intrinsic values. This has huge implications for all those involved in promoting the sharing economy at a time when so much of the public discourse on sharing highlights the growth and success of certain businesses in predominantly monetary terms.

To conclude, there is little doubt that through the time-honoured act of sharing we can strengthen communities, reduce consumption and facilitate the nonmonetary distribution of goods and services—and this can potentially help rebalance an economic system that is increasingly dependent on greed and hyper-consumerism for its continued success. But interpersonal sharing is not enough at a time when humanity is facing what can only be described as a global emergency that includes massive poverty and rising levels of inequality, climate change and the wider ecological crisis, as well as ongoing conflicts over the world's dwindling natural resources.

The process of sharing can only play a transformative role in addressing these crises if we move beyond our egocentric understanding of the sharing economy, and embrace national and global forms of sharing that are facilitated by government bodies in response to urgent social and environmental needs. By being vigilant about how we promote and participate in the sharing economy, we can also guard against the pervasive influence of commerce as it seeks to expand into new markets in a last ditch attempt to preserve the status quo. And by working more closely with the many millions of campaigners and organisations across the world who recognise the transformative potential of economic sharing—whether this is explicitly or implicitly expressed—we can significantly strengthen our chances of establishing an ecologically viable and socially just future for all.

> *"It's not a coincidence that the so-called sharing economy exploded in the aftermath of the financial crisis."*

The Sharing Economy Is Propaganda

Avi Asher-Schapiro

Avi Asher-Schapiro is a Brooklyn-based journalist. In the following viewpoint, Asher-Schapiro argues that most coverage of the sharing economy ignores the fact that the businesses engaged in it are exploiting their workers. The sharing economy is currently unregulated; as a result, companies are able to get away without such hard-won labor rights as paid medical leave, medical benefits, a forty-hour workweek, and workers' compensation benefits, he maintains. Regulation is needed to make companies in the sharing economy behave responsibly toward their employees, Asher-Schapiro claims.

As you read, consider the following questions:

1. According to the viewpoint, how did the income gap widen following the financial crisis?

2. How many new drivers does Asher-Schapiro say Uber brings on each month? What percentage does he say work full time?

3. What are some of the ways that companies such as Uber exploit workers, according to the author?

Taking an Uber is not sharing, just like buying a foot-long meatball sandwich at Subway is not "eating fresh."

Sharing economies do exist: couch surfing, lending your neighbor a power drill, giving your cousin a lift to the airport. But to pay per mile for a ride, per night for a room, or per hour for a house cleaner is no different than paying per loaf at the bakery. That a smartphone or website mediates the exchange does not make it sharing. And it does not change fundamentally the relationship between consumers, laborers, and management.

The managers in this triad—Uber, Homejoy, and TaskRabbit—prefer that politicians and commentators call their business "sharing." At the outset, it's important to dispense with the Orwellian term, because it promotes misunderstanding and bad policy. It leads many to conclude, as Matthew Feeney does, that the primary function of these businesses is to provide "information via their technology to individual providers and consumers."

We do not live in an imaginary world of dormant assets, aimless drivers, and idle house cleaners begging for a Yellow Pages 2.0. A sophisticated public policy response to the "sharing economy" must start with an understanding of the markets and human relations that companies like Uber and Airbnb promote—and the social benefit or cost they might entail.

In reporting on Uber, I found many drivers in Los Angeles who drive full-time to pay rent and feed their families. Executives called these drivers "partners" who can choose their own hours; "entrepreneurs," who essentially start their own "business." The drivers I spoke to found themselves in an entirely different sort of relationship. Uber would cut prices, change work rules, and deactivate drivers at will—leaving many feeling disposable and exploited.

My reporting touched a nerve because coverage of the "sharing economy" up to that point largely ignored the economic realities of these workers, which number in the hundreds of thousands. It makes people uncomfortable to imagine that their happy Uber driver is actually struggling to make ends meet, trading a smile for a 5 star rating.

Feeney doesn't consider the implications of the sharing economy on workers at all. Public policy should, however, put these workers and their economic predicament at the center. Likewise, an honest appraisal of "asset-sharing" platforms like Airbnb must take into account the effect on affordable housing stock, rental rates, and community cohesion (Rachel Monroe has documented the danger Airbnb poses to affordable housing here ["More Guests, Empty Houses," *Slate*, February 13, 2014]).

It's not a coincidence that the so-called sharing economy exploded in the aftermath of the financial crisis. In the first years of the "economic recovery," the top 1% slurped up 121% of the income gains. Now six years later, the stock market booms and corporate profits smash records. Yet working people's wages remain unchanged, and nearly 7 million are stuck in temporary jobs against their will.

Enter Uber.

Evangelists for the sharing economy always talk about how important it is to "disrupt" markets. When I spoke to Uber PR, they told me that introducing GPS-hailing technology to the taxi industry solved inefficiencies, benefiting consumers and drivers alike. Many of the practices of the taxi industry are indefensible, and introducing GPS to car services is a welcome, if minor, disruption.

In the long run, however, if the "sharing economy" is disruptive of anything, it is disruptive of hard-fought labor protections. Uber brings on 40,000 new drivers a month. But to avoid minimum wage laws and liability claims, Uber will not admit that it actually employs these drivers—though around 20% work full time.

Uber then extracts millions of dollars from its drivers' labor and invests in ad campaigns and lobbying efforts to spread to other cities. Right now in New York, if you pull up a map of public transportation on Google, the app offers Uber as an alternative to trains and buses, as if a private car amounts to "public transportation."

In the short term, Uber is encouraging drivers to take out predatory subprime car loans with the Spanish bank Santander. But ultimately, Uber wants to replace drivers with robots, as soon as the technology becomes viable.

Matthew Feeney undoubtedly considers these drivers consenting adults in an economic relationship. And that's true. If you believe in the inherent benevolence of market forces—that desperate workers deserve whatever job appears at the intersection of the labor-supply and labor-demand curve—then the sharing economy should be allowed to run its course.

Thankfully we live in a society that rejects that logic outright. Paid medical leave, workers' compensation, the 40-hour workweek—these are all rights won by working people in the face of strong opposition from corporate interests. The sharing economy is just the latest broadside against these hard-fought labor protections.

Other companies, now smelling the potency of the "sharing" brand, sell themselves as the "Uber for laundry," or the "Uber for child care." All of these companies prey on a pool of desperate workers left out of the economic recovery.

A world in which everything is available on-demand for the wealthy, courtesy of low-wage workers, is neither desirable nor fair. It is actually quite similar to the on-demand economies of cities like Cairo or New Delhi. Anyone who spends time in the developing world knows how easy it is to summon a delivery boy, carpenter, or house cleaner at all hours. This so-called efficiency is the product of a deplorable wealth gap—it's no wonder that San Francisco, the birthplace of Uber, now has income inequality that rivals Rwanda.

In the long run, companies like Uber do the opposite of what they promise. Instead of promoting well-paid flexible work, they bring the informal sector under the centralized control of big tech companies. They pit workers against each other, discouraging unionization and collective bargaining—necessary components of a fair labor-management equilibrium. Lured by dishonest claims of high wages, many drivers sink money into cars they can't afford and keep driving for Uber even when wages fall.

Policy makers should not be ensorcelled by "sharing-economy" propaganda. While Uber is a great deal for Wall Streets—drivers front all the capital and take on all the risk, while investors scrape off profit—it's a bad deal for workers.

Companies that profit from the labor of hundreds of thousands of people should be forced to behave like responsible employers. Thankfully, U.S. District Judge Edward Chen appears poised to do just that. Last month, in a hearing for a class-action suit brought against Uber and Lyft, Chen rejected the companies' claim that drivers are not employees, saying: "If all you were doing is selling an app you could sell it at an app store, but Uber does a little more than that, doesn't it?"

Technology innovators should, of course, be rewarded for their inventive coding. But just imagine if Adobe took 20% of the profits from every music producer who used Adobe Premiere to edit sound. That arrangement would never be tolerated by workers in the knowledge economy, and it should not be tolerated by drivers.

If "sharing-economy" corporations don't want to become employers, they can easily sell their technology to the workers who use it—like everyone else. Government can play a constructive role here by requiring that transportation services be owned by workers' collectives, or at least employ unionized labor. To leave the sharing economy space entirely unregulated, as Feeney suggests, would usher in a dystopian future, where the precariously employed hover over their smartphones waiting to be summoned by someone lucky enough to have a full-time job.

> *"The key aim for a transition to a green economy is to enable economic growth and investment while increasing environmental quality and social inclusiveness."*

A Green Economy Is Key to Sustainable Economic Development

United Nations Environment Programme

The United Nations Environment Programme (UNEP) is the agency of the UN that coordinates its environmental efforts. In the following viewpoint, the UNEP argues that compelling evidence suggests that strong economic and social justification supports the transition to a green economy. In a green economy, the goal of sustainable development is met by combating climate change, eradicating poverty, and creating social equity, the author suggests. The author concludes that sustainable development meets the needs of the present without compromising the ability of future generations to meet their own needs.

United Nations Environment Programme, "Towards a Green Economy: Pathways to Sustainable Development and Poverty Eradication," New York: United Nations Environment Programme, 2011. Copyright © 2011 by United Nations Environment Programme (UNEP). All rights reserved. Reproduced with permission.

As you read, consider the following questions:

1. What are some of the crises that have unfolded during the last decade, according to the UNEP?

2. What is the definition of a "green economy," according to the viewpoint?

3. What enabling conditions will make the transition to a green economy possible, according to the UNEP?

The last two years [2009–2011] have seen the idea of a "green economy" float out of its specialist moorings in environmental economics and into the mainstream of policy discourse. It is found increasingly in the words of heads of state and finance ministers, in the text of G20 [a forum for the finance ministers from twenty major economies] communiques, and discussed in the context of sustainable development and poverty eradication.

This recent traction for a green economy concept has no doubt been aided by widespread disillusionment with the prevailing economic paradigm, a sense of fatigue emanating from the many concurrent crises and market failures experienced during the very first decade of the new millennium, including especially the financial and economic crisis of 2008. But at the same time, there is increasing evidence of a way forward, a new economic paradigm—one in which material wealth is not delivered perforce at the expense of growing environmental risks, ecological scarcities and social disparities.

Mounting evidence also suggests that transitioning to a green economy has sound economic and social justification. There is a strong case emerging for a redoubling of efforts by both governments as well as the private sector to engage in such an economic transformation. For governments, this would include leveling the playing field for greener products by phasing out antiquated subsidies, reforming policies and providing new incentives, strengthening market infrastructure and market-based mechanisms, redirecting public investment, and greening public procurement. For the private sector, this would involve understanding and sizing the true opportunity represented by green economy transitions across a number of key sectors, and responding to policy reforms and price signals through higher levels of financing and investment.

An Era of Capital Misallocation

Several concurrent crises have unfolded during the last decade: climate, biodiversity, fuel, food, water, and more recently, in the global financial system. Accelerating carbon emissions indicate a mounting threat of climate change, with potentially disastrous human consequences. The fuel price shock of 2007–2008 and the related skyrocketing food and commodity prices, reflect both structural weaknesses and unresolved risks. Forecasts by the International Energy Agency (IEA) and others of rising fossil fuel demand and energy prices suggest an ongoing dependence as the world economy struggles to recover and grow.

Currently, there is no international consensus on the problem of global food security or on possible solutions for how to nourish a population of 9 billion by 2050. . . . Freshwater scarcity is already a global problem, and forecasts suggest a growing gap by 2030 between annual freshwater demand and renewable supply. The outlook for improved sanitation still looks bleak for over 1.1 billion people and 844 million people still lack access to clean drinking water. Collectively, these crises are severely impacting the possibility of sustaining prosperity worldwide and achieving the Millennium Development Goals (MDGs) for reducing extreme poverty. They are also compounding persistent social problems, such as job losses, socioeconomic insecurity, disease and social instability.

The causes of these crises vary, but at a fundamental level they all share a common feature: the gross misallocation of capital. During the last two decades, much capital was poured

225

into property, fossil fuels and structured financial assets with embedded derivatives. However, relatively little in comparison was invested in renewable energy, energy efficiency, public transportation, sustainable agriculture, ecosystem and biodiversity protection, and land and water conservation.

Most economic development and growth strategies encouraged rapid accumulation of physical, financial and human capital, but at the expense of excessive depletion and degradation of natural capital, which includes the endowment of natural resources and ecosystems. By depleting the world's stock of natural wealth—often irreversibly—this pattern of development and growth has had detrimental impacts on the well-being of current generations and presents tremendous risks and challenges for the future. The recent multiple crises are symptomatic of this pattern.

Existing policies and market incentives have contributed to this problem of capital misallocation because they allow businesses to run up significant, largely unaccounted for, and unchecked social and environmental externalities. To reverse such misallocation requires better public policies, including pricing and regulatory measures, to change the perverse incentives that drive this capital misallocation and ignore social and environmental externalities. At the same time, appropriate regulations, policies and public investments that foster changes in the pattern of private investment are increasingly being adopted around the world, especially in developing countries. . . .

What Is a Green Economy?

UNEP [United Nations Environment Programme] defines a green economy as one that results in "improved human well-being and social equity, while significantly reducing environmental risks and ecological scarcities". In its simplest expression, a green economy is low carbon, resource efficient, and socially inclusive. In a green economy, growth in income and employment are driven by public and private investments that reduce carbon emissions and pollution, enhance energy and resource efficiency, and prevent the loss of biodiversity and ecosystem services.

These investments need to be catalysed and supported by targeted public expenditure, policy reforms and regulation changes. The development path should maintain, enhance and, where necessary, rebuild natural capital as a critical economic asset and as a source of public benefits. This is especially important for poor people whose livelihoods and security depend on nature.

The key aim for a transition to a green economy is to enable economic growth and investment while increasing environmental quality and social inclusiveness. Critical to attaining such an objective is to create the conditions for public and private investments to incorporate broader environmental and social criteria. In addition, the main indicators of economic performance, such as growth in gross domestic product (GDP) need to be adjusted to account for pollution, resource depletion, declining ecosystem services, and the distributional consequences of natural capital loss to the poor.

A major challenge is reconciling the competing economic development aspirations of rich and poor countries in a world economy that is facing increasing climate change, energy insecurity and ecological scarcity. A green economy can meet this challenge by offering a development path that reduces carbon dependency, promotes resource and energy efficiency and lessens environmental degradation. As economic growth and investments become less dependent on liquidating environmental assets and sacrificing environmental quality, both rich and poor countries can attain more sustainable economic development.

The concept of a green economy does not replace sustainable development; but there is a growing recognition that achieving sustainability rests almost entirely on getting the economy right. Decades of creating new wealth through a "brown economy" model based on fossil fuels have not substantially addressed social marginalisation, environmental degradation and resource depletion. In addition, the world is still far from delivering on the Millennium Development Goals by 2015. . . .

Most interpretations of sustainability take as their starting point the consensus reached by the World Commission on Environment and Development (WCED) in 1987, which defined sustainable development as "development that meets the needs of the present without compromising the ability of future generations to meet their own needs".

Economists are generally comfortable with this broad interpretation of sustainability, as it is easily translatable into economic terms: an increase in well-being today should not result in reducing well-being tomorrow. That is, future generations should be entitled to at least the same level of economic opportunities—and thus at least the same level of economic welfare—as is available to current generations.

As a result, economic development today must ensure that future generations are left no worse off than current generations. Or, as some economists have succinctly expressed it, per capita welfare should not be declining over time. According to this view, it is the total stock of capital employed by the economic system, including natural capital, which determines the full range of economic opportunities, and thus well-being. Society must decide how best to use its total capital stock today to increase current economic activities and welfare. Society must also decide how much it needs to save or accumulate for tomorrow, and ultimately, for the well-being of future generations.

However, it is not simply the aggregate stock of capital in the economy that may matter but also its composition, in particular whether current generations are using up one form of capital to meet today's needs. For example, much of the interest in sustainable development is driven by concern that economic development may be leading to rapid accumulation of physical and human capital at the expense of excessive depletion and degradation of natural capital. The major concern is that by irreversibly depleting the world's stock of natural wealth, today's development path will have detrimental implications for the well-being of future generations. . . .

Moving toward a green economy must become a strategic economic policy agenda for achieving sustainable development. A green economy recognises that the goal of sustainable development is improving the quality of human life within the constraints of the environment, which include combating global climate change, energy insecurity, and ecological scarcity. However, a green economy cannot be focused exclusively on eliminating environmental problems and scarcity. It must also address the concerns of sustainable development with intergenerational equity and eradicating poverty.

A Green Economy and Eradicating Poverty

Most developing countries, and certainly the majority of their populations, depend directly on natural resources. The livelihoods of many of the world's rural poor are also intricately linked with exploiting fragile environments and ecosystems. Well over 600 million of the rural poor currently live on lands prone to degradation and water stress, and in upland areas, forest systems, and drylands that are vulnerable to climatic and ecological disruptions. The tendency of rural populations to be clustered on marginal lands and in fragile environments is likely to be a continuing problem for the foreseeable future, given current global rural population and poverty trends. Despite rapid global urbanisation, the rural population of developing regions continues to grow, albeit at a slower rate in recent decades. Furthermore, around three-quarters of the developing world's poor still live in rural areas, which means about twice as many poor people live in rural rather than in urban areas.

The world's poor are especially vulnerable to the climate-driven risks posed by rising sea levels, coastal erosion and more frequent storms. Around 14 per cent of the population and 21 per cent of urban dwellers in developing countries live in low elevation coastal zones that are exposed to these risks. The livelihoods of billions—from poor farmers to urban slum dwellers—are threatened by a wide range of climate-induced risks that affect food security, water availability, natural disasters, ecosystem stability and human health. For example, many of the 150 million urban inhabitants, who are likely to be at risk from extreme coastal flooding events and sea level rise, are likely to be the poor living in cities in developing countries.

As in the case of climate change, the link between ecological scarcity and poverty is well established for some of the most critical environmental and energy problems. For example, for the world's poor, global water scarcity manifests itself as a water poverty problem. One in five people in the developing world lacks access to sufficient clean water, and about half the developing world's population, 2.6 billion people, do not have access to basic sanitation. More than 660 million of the people without sanitation live on less than US$2 a day, and more than 385 million on less than US$1 a day. . . .

Thus, finding ways to protect global ecosystems, reduce the risks of global climate change, improve energy security, and simultaneously improve the livelihoods of the poor are important challenges in the transition to a green economy, especially for developing countries. . . .

A transition to a green economy can contribute to eradicating poverty. A number of sectors with green economic potential are particularly important for the poor, such as agriculture, forestry, fishery and water management, which have public goods qualities. Investing in greening these sectors, including through scaling up microfinance, is likely to benefit the poor in terms of not only jobs, but also secure livelihoods that are predominantly based on ecosystem services. Enabling the poor to access micro-insurance coverage against natural disasters and catastrophes is equally important for protecting livelihood assets from external shocks due to changing and unpredictable weather patterns. . . .

In sum, the top priority of the UN MDGs is eradicating extreme poverty and hunger, including halving the proportion of people living on less than US$1 a day by 2015. A green economy must not only be consistent with that objective, but must also ensure that policies and investments geared toward reducing environmental risks and scarcities are compatible with ameliorating global poverty and social inequity.

If the desirability of moving to a green economy is clear to most people, the means of doing so is still a work in progress for many. . . .

Enabling Conditions for a Green Economy

To make the transition to a green economy, specific enabling conditions will be required. These enabling conditions consist of national regulations, policies, subsidies and incentives, as well as international market and legal infrastructure, trade and technical assistance. Currently, enabling conditions are heavily weighted toward, and encourage, the prevailing brown economy, which depends excessively on fossil fuels, resource depletion and environmental degradation. . . .

Thus, moving toward a green development path is almost certainly a means for attaining welfare improvements across a society, but it is also often a means for attaining future growth improvement. This is because a shift away from basic production modes of development based on extraction and consumption and toward more complex modes of development can be a good long-term strategy for growth. There are several reasons why this shift might be good for long-term competitiveness as well as for social welfare.

First, employing strong environmental policies can drive inefficiencies out of the economy by removing those firms and industries that only exist because of implicit subsidies in underpriced resources. The free use of air, water and ecosystems is not a valueless good for any actor in an economy and amounts to subsidising negative net worth activities. Introducing effective regulation and market-based mechanisms to contain pollution and limit the accumulation of environmental liabilities drives the economy in a more efficient direction.

Second, resource pricing is important not just for the pricing of natural capital and services, but also for pricing of all the other inputs within an economy. An economy allocates its efforts and expenditures according to relative prices, and underpriced resources result in unbalanced economies. Policy makers should be targeting the future they wish their economies to achieve, and this will usually require higher relative prices on resources. An economy that wishes to develop around knowledge, R&D [research and development], human capital and innovation should not be providing free natural resources.

Third, employing resource pricing drives investments into R&D and innovation. It does so because avoiding costly resources can be accomplished by researching and finding new production methods. This will include investment in all of the factors (human capital and knowledge) and all of the activities (R&D and innovation) listed above. Moving toward more efficient resource pricing is about turning the economy's emphasis toward different foundations of development.

Fourth, these investments may then generate innovation rents. Policies that reflect scarcities that are prevalent in the local economy can also reflect scarcities prevalent more widely. For this reason, a solution to a problem of resource scarcity identified locally (via R&D investments) may have applicability and hence more global marketability. The first solution to a widely experienced problem can be patented, licensed and marketed widely.

Fifth, aggressive environmental regulation may anticipate future widely experienced scarcities and provide a template for other jurisdictions to follow. Such policy leadership can be the first step in the process of innovation, investment, regulation and resource pricing described above.

In sum, the benefits from a strong policy framework to address market failures and ecological scarcities will flow down the environment pathway that comes from altering the direction of an economy. Policies and market-based mechanisms that enhance perceived resource prices create incentives to shift the economy onto a completely different foundation—one based more on investments in innovation and its inputs of human capital, knowledge, and research and development.

| *"Since when has nature, the source of all life, been reduced to a service pro- vider?"*

In a Green Economy, Business Exploits Nature for Profit

Jeff Conant

Jeff Conant is a journalist and the author of A Community Guide to Environmental Health. *In the following viewpoint, Conant maintains that social movements and indigenous people are rejecting the green economy that has emerged following the global economic crisis beginning in 2007. In this far from climate-friendly green economy, corporations and countries are privatizing and exploiting nature for profit, he claims. Policies are being created without the input of indigenous, land-based people, Conant argues, and this is likely to lead to a cycle of poverty and violence.*

As you read, consider the following questions:

1. What did the term "green economy" mean prior to 2007, and what has it come to mean, according to Conant?

2. What is disaster capitalism, according to the viewpoint?

3. What does Conant find particularly offensive about the new green economy?

Everywhere you look these days, things are turning green. In Chiapas, Mexico, indigenous farmers are being paid to protect the last vast stretch of rain forest in Mesoamerica. In the Brazilian Amazon, peasant families are given a monthly "green basket" of basic food staples to allow them to get by without cutting down trees. In Kenya, small farmers who plant climate-hardy trees and protect green zones are promised payment for their part in the fight to reduce global warming. In Mozambique, one of the world's poorest nations, fully 19 percent of the country's surface is leased to a British capital firm that pays families to reforest. These are a few of the keystone projects that make up what is being called "the green economy": an emerging approach that promises to protect planetary ecology while boosting the economy and fighting poverty.

On its face this may sound like a good thing. Yet, during the recently concluded [2012] United Nations [UN] Rio+20 Earth Summit in Brazil, tens of thousands of people attending a nearby People's Summit [the People's Summit for Social and Environmental Justice] condemned such approaches to environmental management. Indeed, if social movements gathered in Rio last month had one common platform, it was "No to the green economy."

Whose Economy? Whose Green?

Just a few years ago, the term "green economy" referred to economies that are locally based, climate friendly, and low impact. But since the global economic meltdown began in 2007, the green economy has come to mean something more akin to the wholesale privatization of nature. This green economy is about putting a price on natural cycles through a controversial set of policies called "Payments for Ecosystem Services"—an approach to greening capitalism that some liken to a tiger claiming to turn vegetarian.

Rather than reducing pollution and consumption, protecting the territorial rights of land-based peoples, and promoting local initiatives that steward resources for future generations, the approach is doing the opposite: promoting monoculture tree plantations, trade in pollution credits, and the establishment of speculative markets in biodiversity and forests, all of which threaten to displace land-based communities.

A report by Ecosystem Marketplace, the leading purveyor of "Payments for Ecosystem Services," lays out the green economy argument: "Ecosystems provide trillions of dollars in clean water, flood protection, fertile lands, clean air, pollination, disease control. . . . So how do we secure this enormously valuable infrastructure and its services? The same way we would electricity, potable water, or natural gas. We pay for it."

The United Nations Environment Programme (UNEP), among the chief proponents of the green economy, says this approach will result in "improved well-being and social equity while significantly reducing environmental risks and ecological scarcities." The World Bank, also promoting the green economy, says, "Natural capital accounting would add to our national GDPs [gross domestic prodcuts] the wealth stored in our natural resources: minerals before they are mined, forests before they are felled, water while it is still in the rivers."

But, for social movements, land-based communities, and indigenous peoples, the question is, who really pays? For what are they paying? And, most poignantly, since when has nature, the source of all life, been reduced to a service provider?

One concern is that this new green economy is a form of "disaster capitalism"—a global effort to put the "services" of nature into the same hands that caused the global financial meltdown. And that seems like a very, very bad idea.

Increasingly, the evidence on the ground bears this out.

The reforestation plan in Mozambique has peasant farmers planting industrial monocultures of African palm for biofuel production, not native forest. The Kenyan farmers of the Green Belt Movement, while initially receptive to a World Bank–backed scheme that would pay them to protect agricultural soils, became discouraged when they realized the payments would add up to less than 15 cents per acre per year, and that they would have to wait many years for payment. In Brazil, the "green basket" of food staples adds up to 100 reales per family per month—but cooking gas alone can cost 50 reales a month, leaving families without access to the forest hungry and dependent on paltry state support.

And in Chiapas, where families in the Lacandon community are paid to protect the forest against their neighbors, the struggling *campesinos* from the Tzeltal, Tzotzil, Choi, and Mam ethnic groups are forced off the land and into prefab peri-urban settlements, where their customs and traditional livelihoods will be forever lost.

Carbon Dumps?

All of these initiatives are based on carbon offsetting—essentially, permission slips purchased by corporations and governments to allow them to continue dumping CO_2 into the atmosphere in exchange for the ecosystem service provided by forests and agricultural soils in the global south, which act as carbon sinks.

But, as Nigerian activist Godwin Ojo says, "Forests are not carbon sinks, they are food baskets." Ojo tells of a rubber plantation near his home that has deprived hundreds of farmers of their livelihood under the auspices of the United Nations Collaborative [Programme] on Reducing Emissions from Deforestation and Forest Degradation, a pillar program of the green economy.

"We find that most policies affecting indigenous peoples are designed without our participation," Ojo says. "If this trend continues, it will lead to a vicious cycle of poverty and violence."

If this is how the new green economy is playing out on the ground, it is no wonder that it has sparked resistance.

Social movements in the global south do not mince words: The invitation for the People's Summit in Rio declared, "Nothing in the 'green economy' questions the current economy based in extraction and fossil fuels, nor the patterns of consumption and industrial production, but extends this economy into new areas, feeding the myth that economic growth can be infinite."

At the People's Summit, spokespeople allied with smallholder farmers, women's organizations, human rights groups, and others debated Achim Steiner, director of the UNEP.

Larissa Packer, a Brazilian lawyer with *Terra de Direitos*, an organization that works to secure land rights for landless communities, was among those who participated.

"Payment for environmental services," Packer said, "posits that the actions of nature—the water cycle, the carbon cycle, the pollination of flowers by bees—are commodities, subject to the law of the market. In essence, such an approach implies the natural enclosure of these 'services,' and, when encoded in legal norms and property rights, the actual enclosure of the natural areas—forests, watersheds, wetlands. . . . Such an approach is akin to the continued enslavement of nature."

She then offered a clear summary of the economics at work: "In the current market," she said, "prices are based on supply and demand, that is, on scarcity. As petroleum becomes scarce, its value goes up. The green economy will follow the same logic. . . . If we put a price on forests, on biodiversity, on other common goods, those prices will be driven up by scarcity. So, for investors in these things, the greater the scarcity of ecosystem services, the greater their value. Where do we think this will lead?"

Steiner responded by saying that, while we may be frustrated with the state of the world, "whether we like it or not, economic thinking is dominating all our nations," and we need to come to terms with this.

"When you say we give a price to nature and automatically it becomes a tradable commodity, I would ask, is it not useful to capture the value of an ecosystem also in economic terms? If countries began to understand how dramatic the value of our ecosystems and resources is to the future of our development prospects, then maybe we would enact laws to protect nature, we would increase protected areas, we would have far more indigenous peoples manage land and reserves, and we would pass far harsher laws to prevent the private sector from engaging in destructive practices."

Steiner's plea, however, left the social movements cold. Speaker upon speaker rose to denounce the green economy as the commodification of life, the final enclosure of the commons, and the largest land grab ever dreamed up by the corporate sector.

Tom Goldtooth, director of the Indigenous Environmental Network, boils it down to "the difference between money-centered Western views and the life-centered indigenous worldview based on the sacred female creation principles of Mother Earth."

On June 21, [2012,] winter solstice in Brazil, a delegation of indigenous people from an encampment called Kari-Oca II near the Rio summit delivered a declaration to UN officials. The declaration, signed by more than 500 indigenous leaders and blessed in a ritual ceremony, took direct aim:

> "The Green Economy is a perverse attempt by corporations, extractive industries, and governments to cash in on Creation by privatizing, commodifying, and selling off the Sacred and all forms of life and the sky, including the air we breathe, the water we drink, and all the genes, plants, traditional seeds, trees, animals, fish, biological and cultural di-

versity, ecosystems and traditional knowledge that make life
on Earth possible and enjoyable."

Life-Affirming Alternatives

What is especially offensive about this new green economy is
that it removes from the table all of the positive, life-affirming
approaches that the social movements of the global south
have been nurturing for decades:

- The solidarity economies, where values and prices are
  set within a local, social context in order to create an
  exchange of goods and services outside of corporate-
  controlled markets;

- Rights-based frameworks that protect women, indigenous peoples, and other vulnerable populations not
  only within the market, but from the market;

- The Rights of Mother Earth, which says that all of life
  has inherent and inalienable rights;

- Territoriality, the notion that land-based people are not
  stewarding "a piece of land like a piece of bread," but a
  sovereign space to call home;

- Climate debt, the idea that northern countries, whose
  prosperity is built on resource extraction, slavery, and
  protectionism, must pay for what they have taken; and

- The Commons, that age-old notion that democratic
  governance of shared resources must happen in spaces
  explicitly protected from the dominance of the market.

In other words, rather than expanding the scope of markets to every domain of nature, a true green economy would
do the opposite: reverse the tide of commodification and fi-
nancialization, reduce the role of markets and the financial
sector, and strengthen democratic control over the world's
ecological commons.

As the Kari-Oca declaration was delivered at the Earth Summit, many of those present looked up to notice a condor circling over the ceremony. In a week filled with acrimony and heated debate, with the United Nations poised to sell off the very foundations of life and our common heritage, the moment was rich with significance. If the social movements are able to stand their ground, that condor, the wind upon which it hovered, and the life which its solstice flight affirmed, will remain ever as it was that day—just out of reach and priceless.

> *"Sustainable development can become a viable future when transnational corporations recognize that with their position of global influence comes responsibility in the societies and environments in which they are embedded."*

Businesses Need to Become Responsible for Sustainable Economic Development

Supriya Kumar

Supriya Kumar is the communications manager of the Worldwatch Institute. In the following viewpoint, Kumar maintains that the current economic model that places the interests of private enterprise ahead of the public good needs to change into a model that will enable sustainable prosperity. Corporations need to recognize it is in their best interests to operate ethically, to protect the environment, and to reduce inequality of income and opportunity, she argues. It is possible to make a profit while operating with environmentally sustainable principles, Kumar concludes.

Supriya Kumar, "Mobilizing the Global Business Community to Achieve Sustainable Prosperity," Worldwatch Institute, November 6, 2012. Copyright © 2012 by Worldwatch Institute. All rights reserved. Reproduced with permission.

As you read, consider the following questions:

1. According to Kumar, what four areas are in need of transformation by the modern corporation?

2. What is wrong with the current economic model, according to Kumar?

3. What are three ideas Kumar posits to bring the world closer to an ideal global economy?

Transnational corporations are now so numerous and in some cases so well capitalized that their global influence now rivals and in many cases exceeds that of governments, according to research published by the Worldwatch Institute.

Around 80,000 transnational corporations (TNCs) operate worldwide, a mere 147 of which control 40 percent of the total value of all these corporations' value. Any vision of a sustainable future must include full recognition of the role that TNCs play in shaping the planet's human and ecological destiny, authors argue in the Worldwatch Institute's *State of the World 2012: Moving Toward Sustainable Prosperity.*

Corporations Have Responsibilities to Society

Because corporations operate with a primary purpose of increasing value for their shareholders, they have often tended to de-prioritize other fundamental concerns. In the worst instances, the pursuit of profit by corporations worldwide has led to neglect for their employees, lack of accountability in their societies, and indifference in their contribution to negative environmental effects. These failures have come under particular scrutiny since the beginning of the financial crisis in 2008 and the realization that financial corporations deemed "too big to fail" pose a serious threat for the economy.

In their chapter, "Reinventing the Corporation," in *State of the World 2012*, Allen White and Monica Baraldi of the Tellus Institute outline four areas of needed transformation for the modern corporation:

- *Purpose.* A company is not required to have a statement of purpose in countries that have common law traditions, including the United States, the United Kingdom, Australia, and Canada. The B Corp (or "benefit" corporation) is a U.S. example where participants are required to have a corporate purpose to create material positive impact on society and the environment.

- *Ownership.* Ownership systems such as trust ownership, hybrid social enterprises, and cooperative ownership have much more potential to align their goals and values for the benefit of society and to realize that their actions form part of the larger economic system. These alternative ownership structures are flourishing around the world and provide testament to the ability of corporations to operate successfully while contributing to the benefit of society.

- *Capital.* Historically, capital markets operated without regard to long-term social or environmental impacts or regulations. Recent efforts to embed sustainability within the investment decision-making process show that it is possible to generate significant changes in corporate sustainability behavior.

- *Governance.* If boards can shift from a narrow focus on increasing shareholder value to a more comprehensive view of the corporation and its impacts, progress toward sustainable development can be achieved. While far from sufficient, corporate reporting is a first step in improving governance through increased transparency and long-term goal setting.

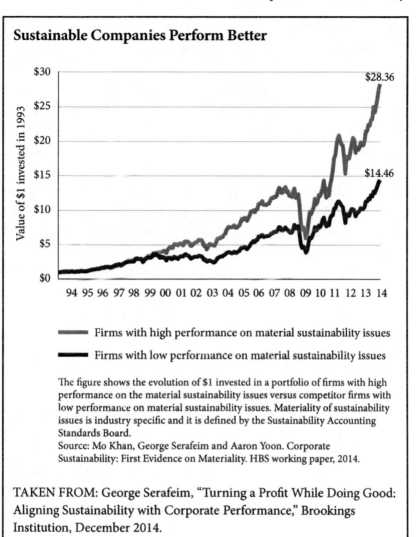

Sustainable Companies Perform Better

Firms with high performance on material sustainability issues

Firms with low performance on material sustainability issues

The figure shows the evolution of $1 invested in a portfolio of firms with high performance on the material sustainability issues versus competitor firms with low performance on material sustainability issues. Materiality of sustainability issues is industry specific and it is defined by the Sustainability Accounting Standards Board.
Source: Mo Khan, George Serafeim and Aaron Yoon. Corporate Sustainability: First Evidence on Materiality. HBS working paper, 2014.

TAKEN FROM: George Serafeim, "Turning a Profit While Doing Good: Aligning Sustainability with Corporate Performance," Brookings Institution, December 2014.

In critically thinking about corporations, it is necessary to remember that they are not islands: Corporations operate within a vast economic system that includes a multitude of players and variables. Sustainable development can become a viable future when transnational corporations recognize that with their position of global influence comes responsibility to the societies and environments in which they are embedded.

A New Economic Model Is Needed

The current global economic model is socially narrow and environmentally predatory, placing private interests above public ones. As such, it is unable to address the dire needs of a world burdened by a population of 7 billion people, let alone the looming threat of climate change and alarming levels of poverty. What is needed is a new economic model that draws from a new paradigm of development that is not based solely on economic growth but rather integrates and embraces the natural limits of our planet, the need for reducing inequalities of income and opportunity, ethical principles, and the preservation of the rights of future generations.

In their *State of the World 2012* chapter, "Mobilizing the Business Community in Brazil and Beyond," authors Jorge Abrahão, Paulo Itacarambi, and Henrique Lian (all members of the governing body of the Ethos Institute) advocate for internalizing a variety of multilateral commitments to bring the world closer to the ideal global economy. These include [the following:]

Payment for Ecosystem Services. Natural resources and environmental services should come with a quantifiable, concrete price tag in order to change perceptions and the way markets function. The goal is to close the production loop—by using renewable energy inputs and generating no waste outputs—and to fully acknowledge the shared benefits from biodiversity.

Establishment of Minimum Operation Standards. Businesses—domestic and international alike—should be required to obey a certain set of standards that governs decent work, inclusion of minorities, socio-environmental practices, sustainable development, and closed-loop production.

Promotion of Sustainable Production and Consumption. Governments must take the lead in lifting the pressure off natural resources, cutting carbon emissions, and facilitating decent work conditions through innovative strategies such as sustainable government procurement policies, research and development programs, and tax regimes. This in turn can encourage sustainable production patterns that are effectively paired with behavioral changes that start with the consumer.

"*Despite perceptions that 'sustainable business' is up and running, the environment reminds us we're failing to deal with the problem at anywhere near sufficient scale.*"

Businesses Are Ignoring Key Barriers to Global Sustainability

Auden Schendler and Michael Toffel

Auden Schendler is vice president of sustainability at Aspen Skiing Company and the author of Getting Green Done: Hard Truths from the Front Lines of the Sustainability Revolution. *Michael Toffel is associate professor of business administration at Harvard Business School. In the following viewpoint, Schendler and Toffel argue that although many companies are trumpeting their green initiatives, most of their efforts do not address the central issue of climate change. Despite their best efforts, even the largest businesses do not have the power to impact climate change, the authors maintain. Since only governments can provide the systemic approach that is needed, businesses should lobby for climate legislation, Schendler and Toffel conclude.*

As you read, consider the following questions:

1. According to the viewpoint, without action on climate change, what will happen to global temperatures by 2100, and what will be the impact?

2. What are the five elements needed for a meaningful corporate sustainability program, according to the authors?

3. According to the viewpoint, what are Nike and Starbucks doing to address climate change?

Green initiatives are ubiquitous these days, implemented with zeal at companies like DuPont, IBM, Walmart, and [the] Walt Disney [Company]. The programs being rolled out—lighting retrofits, zero-waste factories, and carpool incentives—save money and provide a green glow. Most large companies are working to reduce energy use and waste, and many have integrated sustainability into strategic planning. What's not to like?

Green Initiatives Fail to Address Climate Change

Well, for starters, these actions don't meaningfully address the primary barrier to sustainability, climate change. According to the International Energy Agency, without action, global temperatures will likely increase 6 degrees C [Celsius] by 2100, "which would have devastating consequences for the planet." This means more super droughts, floods, storms, fires, crop failures, sea level rise, and other major disruptions. "Sustainability" simply isn't possible in the face of such a problem, as Superstorm Sandy [a hurricane in 2012] demonstrated.

So despite perceptions that "sustainable business" is up and running, the environment reminds us we're failing to deal with the problem at anywhere near sufficient scale. Because climate change requires a systemic solution, which only governments can provide, firms serious about addressing it have a critical role well beyond greening their own operations. They must spur government action. But few are.

"Green business" as currently practiced focuses on limited operational efficiencies—cutting carbon footprints and waste reduction—and declares victory. But these measures fail to even dent the climate problem. And the proof is easy: Greenhouse gas emissions continue to rise. Last month [May 2013], we hit 400 parts per million atmospheric CO_2 for the first time in 3 million years. Worse, though, such small-ball initiatives are a distraction: We fiddle around the edges thinking we're making a real difference (and getting accolades), while the planet inexorably warms.

The reality is that even if one company eliminates its carbon footprint entirely—as Microsoft admirably pledged to do—global warming roars on. That's because the problem is too vast for any single business: Solving climate change means we must switch to mostly carbon-free energy sources by 2050 or find a way to affordably capture carbon dioxide emissions, both monumental tasks.

Even several very large companies cannot, on their own, get us there. In fact, historically, no big environmental problem—from air and water pollution to acid rain or ozone depletion—has ever been solved by businesses volunteering to do the right thing. We ought not presume that voluntary measures will solve this one.

But nobody seems to have noticed. Most green scorecards, corporate strategies, media, and shareholder analyses of businesses focus almost entirely on operational greening activities and policies, but not on whether companies can continue on their current course in a climate-changed world. In other words, such analyses don't actually measure sustainability.

A Meaningful Corporate Sustainability Program

So what does a meaningful corporate sustainability program look like in the era of climate change?

First, corporate leaders need to directly lobby state and national politicians to introduce sweeping, aggressive bipartisan climate legislation such as a carbon fee-and-dividend program. Strong policy in G8 nations [a group of eight leading industrial nations] is all the more important because it removes excuses for inaction by China, India, and other countries with rapidly growing carbon footprints.

Second, CEOs [chief executive officers] should insist that trade groups prioritize climate policy activism and withdraw from associations that refuse to do so, like when Pacific Gas and Electric, Apple, and Nike left the U.S. Chamber of Commerce over its opposition to regulating greenhouse gas emissions.

Third, businesses should market their climate activism so that customers and suppliers appreciate their leadership, understand what matters, and follow suit. Such marketing is also education on one of the key issues of our time.

Fourth, companies should partner with effective nongovernmental organizations such as the Coalition for Environmentally Responsible Economies, the Natural Resources Defense Council, 350.org, Protect Our Winters, and Citizens' Climate Lobby to support their work, become educated on climate science and policy solutions, and understand effective lobbying.

Fifth, managers should demand that suppliers assess their climate impact and set public targets to reduce greenhouse gas emissions. But companies that are multiplying their influence in supply chains—like Dell and Walmart—must not miss the larger and more important opportunity to change the rules of the game through activism.

Some Companies Are Leading the Way

Even in the United States, a climate laggard, some companies are already responding to climate change in the appropriate way.

Nike, for example, moved beyond operational greening by helping to create BICEP (Business for Innovative Climate and Energy Policy), which brings its members to Washington, D.C., to lobby for aggressive energy and climate legislation.

Starbucks has also taken out full-page ads in major newspapers to raise public awareness about the importance of climate action and has lobbied the U.S. Congress and the [Barack] Obama administration to explain the threat climate poses to coffee.

These companies are the exception. Unfortunately, even businesses that are sustainability leaders—like clothing manufacturer Patagonia, a business we admire—don't recognize the primacy of climate change. Instead, it includes climate in a basket of equally weighted issues, like protecting oceans, forests, or fisheries. But that's misguided: Climate vastly trumps (and often includes) those other environmental concerns.

Businesses that claim to be green but aren't loudly making their voices heard on the need for government action on climate change are missing the point. They are not just dodging the key challenge of sustainability; they are distracting us from what really matters.

Periodical and Internet Sources Bibliography

The following articles have been selected to supplement the diverse views presented in this chapter.

Douglas Beale   "Why Well-Being, Not Just GDP Growth, Should Be the Goal," *Huffington Post*, June 26, 2015.

Koen Frenken, Toon Meelen, Martijn Arets, and Pieter van de Glind   "Smarter Regulation for the Sharing Economy," *Guardian*, May 20, 2015.

Diana Furchtgott-Roth   "Green Jobs in the U.S. Economy," Manhattan Institute for Policy Research, June 6, 2012.

Anthony B. Kim and Brett Schaefer   "Why the 169 Targets UN Is Pursuing Won't Lead to Progress in Reducing Poverty," *Daily Signal*, April 13, 2015.

Annabel Lau   "Dip into the Sharing Economy for Convenience, Community and Extra Cash," *Forbes*, June 3, 2015.

Christopher Mims   "How Everyone Gets the 'Sharing' Economy Wrong," *Wall Street Journal*, May 24, 2015.

Ron Schultz   "Can Sustainable Business and Economic Development Work Together?," *GreenBiz*, September 6, 2013.

Eyob Tadelle   "Ethiopia: Country's Green Economy—Making Sustainable Development a Reality," *Ethiopian Herald*, June 25, 2015.

Gillian B. White   "In the Sharing Economy, No One's an Employee," *Atlantic*, June 8, 2015.

Junjie Zhang   "Is Environmentally Sustainable Economic Growth Possible in China?," *Diplomat*, January 10, 2013.

For Further Discussion

Chapter 1

1. One of the controversies surrounding genetically modified foods is the question of whether or not labeling should be mandatory. Proponents of labeling claim people have a right to know what is in their food. Do you believe genetically modified foods should be labeled? Why, or why not?

2. Madeline Ostrander and David Weisser take the position that genetically modified foods have an important role to play in addressing the global food crisis, while John Robbins and Samuel Fromartz argue that genetically modified foods are not the answer. What do you perceive to be some of the pros and cons of genetically modified foods? Do you believe genetically modified foods can help address world hunger? Explain your reasoning.

Chapter 2

1. The United Nations contends that water is at the core of sustainable development. How does water scarcity threaten sustainable development, and what are some measures that can be taken to ensure a more water secure world?

2. Sammy Roth writes that desalination is an answer to California's water crisis, while Aaron Lada contends that desalination is not a viable solution to the world's water problems. What do you perceive to be some of the pros and cons of desalination? Do you believe desalination can play an effective role in combatting water scarcity? Explain.

Chapter 3

1. In its report "A New Global Partnership," the United Nations sets forth the position that the eradication of poverty is necessary for global sustainability. Brett D. Schaefer and Ambassador Terry Miller argue that a focus on poverty is the wrong way of going about promoting economic growth. What are some of the goals each viewpoint is setting forth? Do you think these goals are in conflict? Why, or why not? Explain.

2. Sneha Barot argues that providing effective contraceptive services to women worldwide would save lives and money. Steven W. Mosher contends that the United Nations' agenda on gender equality amounts to an assault on marriage and the family. How do Barot's and Mosher's arguments relate to the issue of global sustainability? Explain your reasoning.

Chapter 4

1. The sustainability of economic growth is debated in viewpoints by John de Graaf and Ronald Bailey. The former argues that economic growth is not sustainable, while the latter makes a case that sustainability can exist under free market capitalism. What are some of the ways in which economic growth makes a contribution to sustainability? What are some of the problems it creates for sustainability? Do you believe that free market capitalism can mitigate some of these problems? Why, or why not?

2. Rajesh Makwana maintains that the sharing economy is necessary for global sustainability, while Avi Asher-Schapiro contends that companies in the sharing economy exploit their workers. What are some of the companies in the sharing economy? Have you ever used any of their services? Would you be inclined to? Why, or why not?

Organizations to Contact

The editors have compiled the following list of organizations concerned with the issues debated in this book. The descriptions are derived from materials provided by the organizations. All have publications or information available for interested readers. The list was compiled on the date of publication of the present volume; the information provided here may change. Be aware that many organizations take several weeks or longer to respond to inquiries, so allow as much time as possible.

Center for the Advancement of the Steady State Economy (CASSE)
5101 South Eleventh Street, Arlington, VA   22204
(703) 901-7190
e-mail: info@steadystate.org
website: www.steadystate.org

The mission of the Center for the Advancement of the Steady State Economy (CASSE) is to advance the steady state economy, with stabilized population and consumption, as a policy goal with widespread public support. The activities of CASSE are to educate citizens and policy makers on the benefits of the steady state economy, promote the steady state economy as a desirable alternative to economic growth, and to study the means to establish a steady state economy. Links to briefing papers published by CASSE are available on its website.

Center for Sustainable Economy (CSE)
16869 SW Sixty-Fifth Avenue, Suite 493
Lake Oswego, OR   97035-7865
(503) 657-7336
e-mail: info@sustainable-economy.org
website: www.sustainable-economy.org

The Center for Sustainable Economy (CSE) is an environmental economics think tank whose goal is to speed the transition to a sustainable society. CSE analyzes the impacts of public policy, programs, and projects; proposes solutions; and provides support for legislative, administrative, and legal campaigns. Included on the CSE website are updates, commentary, and blog posts on such topics as land use and climate economics.

Foundation for Sustainable Development (FSD)

1000 Brannan Street, Suite 207, San Francisco, CA 94103

(415) 283-4873

e-mail: info@fsdinternational.org

website: www.fsdinternational.org

The Foundation for Sustainable Development (FSD) is an international, nonprofit research and consultancy foundation that coordinates projects such as the Ecosystem Services Partnership that are designed to support the conservation and sustainable use of natural ecosystems. The areas of expertise of FSD are ecosystem assessment and nature valuation, biodiversity and climate change, communication and capacity building, and ecosystem management and restoration.

Guttmacher Institute

125 Maiden Lane, 7th Floor, New York, NY 10038

(212) 248-1111 • fax: (212) 248-1951

website: www.guttmacher.org

The mission of the Guttmacher Institute is to advance sexual and reproductive health and rights through an interrelated program of research, policy analysis, and public education designed to generate new ideas, encourage enlightened public debate, and promote sound policy and program development. The institute produces a wide range of publications on topics pertaining to sexual and reproductive health, including the journal *Perspectives on Sexual and Reproductive Health* and the public policy journal *Guttmacher Policy Review*.

International Organization for Sustainable Development (IOSD)
1250 Twenty-Fourth Street NW, Suite 300
Washington, DC 20037
(202) 263-3628 • fax: (202) 466-0502
e-mail: info@iosd.org
website: www.iosd.org

The mission of the International Organization for Sustainable Development (IOSD) is to foster the well-being of all human beings by promoting sustainable economic development, encouraging intercultural dialogue, and facilitating access to world-class higher education, especially in the developing nations of Africa and the Pacific. The IOSD publishes academic papers on sustainable development that can be accessed on its website.

Partnership for Sustainable Communities (PSC)
1200 New Jersey Avenue SE, Washington, DC 21509
(202) 366-4416
e-mail: livability@dot.gov
website: www.sustainablecommunities.gov

The Partnership for Sustainable Communities (PSC) is an interagency partnership of the US Department of Housing and Urban Development, the US Department of Transportation, and the US Environmental Protection Agency. PSC works to coordinate federal housing, transportation, water, and other infrastructure investments to make neighborhoods more prosperous, allow people to live closer to jobs, save households time and money, and reduce pollution.

United Nations (UN)
405 East Forty-Second Street, New York, NY 10017
(212) 963-1234
website: www.un.org

The United Nations (UN) is an international organization made up of 193 member countries. The charter of the UN is to maintain international peace and security, promote sustainable development, protect human rights, and uphold international law. A sustainable development agenda, "2015: Time for Global Action for People and Planet," was launched by the UN in an effort to end poverty, promote prosperity and well-being for all, protect the environment, and address climate change. The UN publishes extensively on sustainable development with reports such as "A New Global Partnership: Eradicate Poverty and Transform Economies Through Sustainable Development."

World Bank

1818 H Street NW, Washington, DC   20433

(202) 473-1000

website: www.worldbank.org

The World Bank is an international financial institution that provides loans to developing countries as well as advice and research to aid their economic development. The World Bank has set two goals to achieve by 2030: to end extreme poverty by decreasing the percentage of people living on less than $1.25 a day, and to promote shared prosperity by fostering the income growth of the bottom 40 percent for every country. The World Bank creates a number of publications dealing with global sustainability that can be accessed on its website.

World Resources Institute (WRI)

10 G Street NE, Suite 800, Washington, DC   20002

(202) 729-7600 • fax: (202) 729-7686

website: www.wri.org

The World Resources Institute (WRI) is a global research organization whose work is focused on the environment and sustainable development. WRI does research on six issues: climate, energy, food, forests, water, and sustainable cities. The WRI website offers reports, working papers, issue briefs, and fact sheets, as well as features the *Insights* blog with entries on the environment, human development, and global sustainability.

Worldwatch Institute

1400 Sixteenth Street NW, Suite 430, Washington, DC   20036
(202) 745-8092 • fax: (202) 478-2534
website: www.worldwatch.org

The Worldwatch Institute is a nonprofit organization that works to accelerate the transition to a sustainable world that meets human needs. The main objectives of the institute are universal access to renewable energy and nutritious food, expansion of environmentally sound jobs and development, transformation of cultures from consumerism to sustainability, and an early end to population growth through healthy and intentional childbearing. The institute publishes books, reference guides, reports, the magazine *World Watch*, and the annual "State of the World" report.

Bibliography of Books

Anthony B. Atkinson — *Inequality: What Can Be Done?* Cambridge, MA: Harvard University Press, 2015.

Edward B. Barbier and Anil Markandya — *A New Blueprint for a Green Economy.* New York: Routledge, 2013.

Lester R. Brown — *Full Planet, Empty Plates: The New Geopolitics of Food Scarcity.* New York: W.W. Norton & Company, 2012.

Colin Chartres and Samyuktha Varma — *Out of Water: From Abundance to Scarcity and How to Solve the World's Water Problems.* Upper Saddle River, NJ: Pearson Education, 2011.

Robin Chase — *Peers Inc: How People and Platforms Are Inventing the Collaborative Economy and Reinventing Capitalism.* New York: PublicAffairs, 2015.

Brahma Chellaney — *Water, Peace, and War: Confronting the Global Water Crisis.* Lanham, MD: Rowman & Littlefield Publishers, 2013.

Steven Druker — *Altered Genes, Twisted Truth: How the Venture to Genetically Engineer Our Food Has Subverted Science, Corrupted Government, and Systematically Deceived the Public.* Salt Lake City, UT: Clear River Press, 2015.

Stephen Emmott   *Ten Billion.* New York: Vintage, 2013.

Susan T. Gooden   *Race and Social Equity: A Nervous Area of Government.* New York: Routledge, 2014.

Janet C. Gornick and Markus Jäntti, eds.   *Income Inequality: Economic Disparities and the Middle Class in Affluent Countries.* Stanford, CA: Stanford University Press, 2013.

Tapio Kanninen   *Crisis of Global Sustainability.* New York: Routledge, 2013.

Laura Lengnick   *Resilient Agriculture: Cultivating Food Systems for a Changing Climate.* Gabriola Island, Canada: New Society Publishers, 2015.

Robert Paarlberg   *Food Politics: What Everyone Needs to Know.* New York: Oxford University Press, 2010.

Brian Richter   *Chasing Water: A Guide for Moving from Scarcity to Sustainability.* 2nd ed. Washington, DC: Island Press, 2014.

Pamela C. Ronald and Raoul W. Adamchak   *Tomorrow's Table: Organic Farming, Genetics, and the Future of Food.* New York: Oxford University Press, 2010.

Jeffrey D. Sachs   *The Age of Sustainable Development.* New York: Columbia University Press, 2015.

Takamitsu Sawa, Susumu Iai, and Seiji Ikkatai, eds.   *Achieving Global Sustainability: Policy Recommendations.* New York: United Nations University Press, 2011.

Hans Joachim Schellnhuber et al., eds. *Global Sustainability: A Nobel Cause.* New York: Cambridge University Press, 2010.

David Sedlak *Water 4.0: The Past, Present, and Future of the World's Most Vital Resource.* New Haven, CT: Yale University Press, 2014.

Alex Stephany *The Business of Sharing: Making It in the New Sharing Economy.* New York: Palgrave Macmillan, 2015.

James A.F. Stoner and Charles Wankel, eds. *Global Sustainability as a Business Imperative.* New York: Palgrave Macmillan, 2010.

Akimasa Sumi, Nobuo Mimura, and Toshihiko Masui, eds. *Climate Change and Global Sustainability: A Holistic Approach.* New York: United Nations University Press, 2011.

Gernot Wagner and Martin L. Weitzman *Climate Shock: The Economic Consequences of a Hotter Planet.* Princeton, NJ: Princeton University Press, 2015.

Karl Weber, ed. *Last Call at the Oasis: The Global Water Crisis and Where We Go from Here.* New York: PublicAffairs, 2012.

Benno Werlen, ed. *Global Sustainability: Cultural Perspectives and Challenges for Transdisciplinary Integrated Research.* New York: Springer, 2015.

Index

U